MatarProductions:
MatarTV
MatarEducation
MatarPodcast
Stand February 2020

Copyright © 2020 by Ali Matar
All rights reserved. This book or any portion thereof
may not be reproduced or used in any manner whatsoever
without the express written permission of the publisher
except for the use of brief quotations in a book review.

Ali Matar

Lebanese Arabic:
The Easy Way to Learn Lebanese Grammar

The Ultimate Guide to
Become a Lebanese in the Past, Present and Future

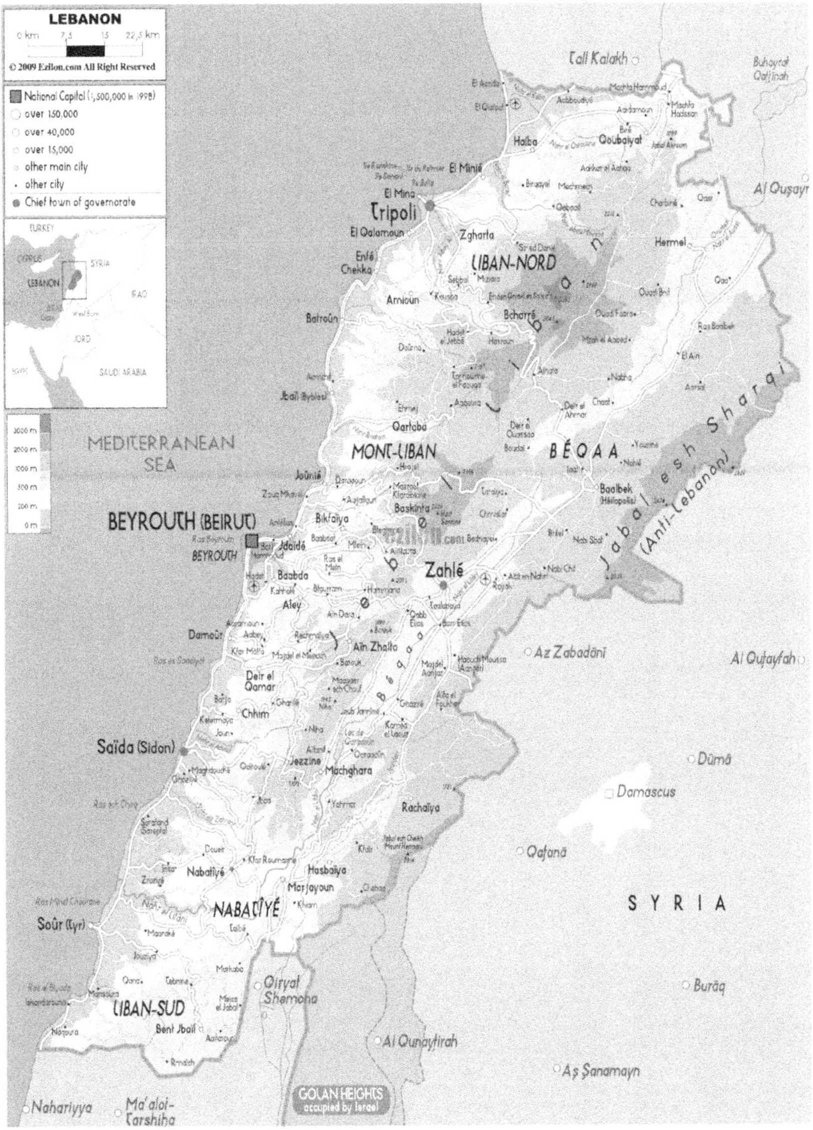
LEBANON
0 km 7,5 15 22,5 km
© 2009 Ezilon.com All Right Reserved
National Capital
over 150,000
over 40,000
over 15,000
other main city
other city
Chief town of governorate
TURKEY
CYPRUS
SYRIA
LEBANON
IRAQ
JORD
SAUDI ARABIA
3000 m
2000 m
1000 m
500 m
200 m
0 m
MEDITERRANEAN SEA
BEYROUTH (BEIRUT)
BEYROUTH
Tall Kalakh
Halba
Qoubaiyat
El Minié
El Mina
Tripoli
El Qalamoun
Zgharta
LIBAN-NORD
Enfé
Chekka
Amioun
Batroûn
Bcharré
Hermel
Al Quşayr
Baalbek
Jbail (Byblos)
Qartaba
MONT-LIBAN
BÉQAA
Jabal esh Sharqi
(Anti-Lebanon)
Joûnié
Bikfaiya
Baskinta
Jdaidé
Baabda
Zahlé
Aley
Damoûr
Aïn Zhalta
Deir el Qamar
Chhim
Saïda (Sidon)
Jezzine
Machghara
Rachaïya
Az Zabadānī
Al Quţayfah
Dūmā
Damascus
Qaţanā
SYRIA
Nabatiyé
Hasbaïya
Marjayoun
NABATIYÉ
Soûr (Tyr)
Qiryat Shemona
LIBAN-SUD
Bent Jbail
Al Qunayţirah
Burāq
Aş Şanamayn
GOLAN HEIGHTS
occupied by Israel
Nahariyya
Ma'alot-Tarshiha

Table of Contents

Pronunciation Guide and Arabic letters in Internet Language . 8

Subject Pronouns 11

The base form 15

The Imperfect Tense 18

The Bi-Imperfect 20

The Active Participle 23

Compound Tenses 24

Verb Conjugations 25

Outro 113

Pronunciation Guide and Arabic letters in Internet Language

A new writing style spreads around the world, especially the Arab world; it's not Arabic or English. It's a mixture between both of them. It has its own name depending on the language by which person transliterate Arabic.

The broader phenomenon is known as Franco Arab.

The roots of this phenomenon go back to 1990 when the western text communication technologies became increasingly prevalent in the Arab world such as personal computers, cellular phones, emails and worldwide webs. At that time, Arabic alphabet wasn't an optional feature and Latin alphabet was commonly used in all of these forms of communication. So, how could Arab users of this new western system communicate?

Written Arabic has 28 letters, some of them include sounds that are not used in English. Arabs had no choice but transliterating their Arabic into English using Latin letters. Not only letters were used in this process but also numbers because some Arabic letters don't have an approximate phonetic equivalent in Latin script. So, they used numerals and other characters to express their Arabic letters, e.g. number "3" is used to stand for the Arabic letter "ع" (Ayn) as they look alike.

Franco Arabic writing features:

For pronunciation purposes, please check my YouTube channel: MatarEducation

Letter	Arabic	Pronunciation	Explanation
2	ء	Glottal Stop	Like you're about to vomit but nothing comes out
Th/s	ث	Thh	The sound effect of a human being impersonating a snake (Throw)
3	ع	Ayn	
5	خ	Kh	Like DJ Khaled, but more a vulgar pronunciation
7	ح	Hh	When you have a sore throat
8/gh	غ	Ghein	

This new writing style on the internet became so popular, it is now used to express everyday speech. Many abbreviations for this speech are invented by the users.

Note: It is really important that you take your time to learn and practice the pronunciations.

Other abbreviations are made up for the most commonly used English expressions in Arab world:

Full	Abbreviation
Laugh out loud	Lol
Welcome back	WB
Tomorrow	Tom
Today	2day
Please	Plz
Before	B4
Blackberry me	Bbm
Facebook me	Fbm
How are you	Hru
How are things	Hrt
See you tomorrow	Cu tom

PS. This is a spoken language not a written one, so writings may differ if you check somewhere else or even later in this book.

Again, for pronunciation purposes, please check my YouTube channel: MatarEducation

Some info adapted from: https://arabeya.wordpress.com/2011/04/27/franco-3arabi/

Subject Pronouns

Also called **personal pronouns**. Arabic subject pronouns tell you who is doing the action of a sentence.

In English, subject pronouns are words such as "you", "we" and "it".

Arabic, is slightly more complicated, because it uses **gender** and **duality**. However, in Lebanese Arabic, duality is not commonly used, only the singularity and plurality are used. For example, "you" can be translated in different ways, depending on who you are talking to. In the case of talking to a singular male, it translates as "**2enta**", but for a singular female "**2ente**".

Normally, if you're talking to two males or two females, it becomes '2antoma'. However, this is not used in the Lebanese Arabic.

And finally, in the Arabic language, if you're talking to a group of three people or more with at least one male, "you" translates as (2antom) and for a group of three or more females (2anton). However, in the Lebanese Arabic, we use „**2ento**" for both males and females. (Life's easier when it's Lebanese Arabic right?)

PS. The subject pronoun "it" does not exist neither in official Arabic language nor the Lebanese Arabic.

Subject Pronouns in English	Subject Pronouns in Lebanese Arabic
I	Ana
You (Male)	2enta/Enta
You (Female)	2ente/Ente
He	Howwe
She	Hiyye
We	Ne7na
You (Plural)	2ento/Ento
They	Hinne

Is and are, are auxiliary verbs that are mainly used in forming the tenses of other verbs.

In the Arabic language, there **are no auxiliary verbs.**

Example:

I am sick → Ana mareed. (I sick, which means I am sick)

Ana: I
*Mareed: **sick***

The correct translation from English to Arabic would be: I ~~am~~ sick.

How to figure out the gender of the noun:

As it has been mentioned before, in the Arabic language, there are feminine and masculine nouns. How do you differ between them? I will tell you a trick that works on almost all nouns.

I will make it as simple as possible:

The nouns ending with:

-a/e *are* <u>feminine</u>
When the pronunciation (the sound) **has a stop** *at the end, it's* <u>masculine.</u>

Example:

Table: Tawle – feminine
Pen: 2alam – masculine

Paper: War2a – feminine
Door: Beb – masculine

Chapters specifically about nouns will be found later in the book. However, I would like to use some of the nouns already in some texts after some chapters to help you comprehend the idea faster.

Text:

Mar7aba. Ana Jean. Howwe 5ayye w hiyye 2i5te. Ne7na 3anna bet. Fi 3anna jnayne kbire. Jiranna ktir mne7. Hinne 3andon Seyyara.

Translation:

Hello. I am jean. He is my brother and she is my sister. We have a house. We have a big garden. Our neighbors are really nice. They have a car.

Nouns:

Bet: *House **(Masculine)***
Jnayne: *Garden **(Feminine)***
Seyyara: *Car **(Feminine)***

The base form

The base form is the most basic form of a verb, free of any prefixes or suffixes.

In both Arabic and English, the base form is the form of a verb listed in dictionary entries. In English, this is the infinitive (**be, go, have, etc…**).

In Arabic, the base form is the **third-person masculine singular** (**howwe**) of the perfect tense. So, although the verb "ra7", for example, might literally mean 'he went' in a sentence, when cited in isolation, its translation would be *'go'* or *'to go'*, the infinitive.

Let's start with the present, present continuous and in one case, the active participle.

Nem: to sleep

Subject Pronouns English	Subject Pronouns Arabic	Present	Present Continuous
I	Ana	Bnem	3am nem
You (m)	Enta	Bitnem	3am tnem
You (f)	Ente	Bitneme	3am tneme
He	Howwe	Binem	3am ynem
She	Hiyye	Bitnem	3am tnem
You (pl)	Ento	Bitnemo	3am tnemo
We	Ne7na	Minnem	3am nnem
They	Hinne	Binemo	3am ynemo

If you want to express a habitual meaning (that you do something regularly), you have to use the present tense. And if you want to express a present continuous meaning (that you "are doing" something right now), you often use present continuous tense, although sometimes you must use the active participle instead.

The past (perfect) tense

For the appropriate verb conjugations, see the past tense (L maade) conjugations here. **Usage of the past tense in the Lebanese Arabic is fairly simple; you use it as much as you would in English.**

Subject Pronouns English	Subject Pronouns Arabic	Present	Past
I	Ana	Bnem	Nemet
You (m)	Enta	Bitnem	Nemet
You (f)	Ente	Bitneme	Nimte
He	Howwe	Binem	Nem
She	Hiyye	Bitnem	Nemit
You (pl)	Ento	Bitnemo	Nemto
We	Ne7na	Minnem	Nemna
They	Hinne	Binemo	Nemo

The Imperfect Tense

Form:

While the perfect tense is conjugated using suffixes, the imperfect tense uses prefixes.

The imperfect prefixes and suffixes are not added to the base form but an imperfect stem.

Use:

- The imperfect can follow an auxiliary. An auxIllary can be an active participle, conjugated - verb, or other certain types of words. The equivalent in English is modal verbs and others that can precede a second verb (which is infinitive or gerund). For example, can go, want to eat, like dancing. In these examples, can, want, and like function as auxiliaries.
- The imperfect is also used to express the future when preceded by the particle "ra7" or the prefixed particle "7a".
- The imperfect follows the progressive particle "3am", equivalent to the present continuous tense of English. It refers to actions happening at the time of speaking, as well as those that are repetitive or ongoing.
- A negative imperative is expressed by placing "ma" in front of a second-person imperfect verb.
- An imperfect verb follows certain conjunctions of purpose and time

It can also be combined with the verb "**Ken**" which means "**I used to...**" or to refer to an action that was taking place in the past. *(ex. was doing)*

Example: I used to write: **Ana kenet 2ektob**

However, the verb "**ken**" also changes according to the pronoun.

Pronouns	Used to: Ken	To write: 2ektob
Ana	Kenet	2ektob
Enta	Kenet	Tektob
Ente	Kente	Teketbe
Howwe	Ken	Yiktob
Hiyye	Kenit	Tiktob
Ento	Kento	Teketbo
Ne7na	Kenna	Niktob
Hinne	Keno	Yeketbo

The Bi-Imperfect

Form:

The Bi-Imperfect is formed by prefixing 'b' to conjugations in the imperfect tense.

Use:

- The Bi-Imperfect tense most often corresponds to the present simple tense of English, referring to general truths and habits.
- The Bi-imperfect can also refer to future, especially to convey intentions.
- The progressive article '3am' is usually followed by a bare imperfect verb, but can, less commonly, precede a Bi-imperfect verb.
- The Bi-imperfect is sometimes interchangeable with the imperfect. Their uses may vary among native speakers, not only from region to region but within the same region, as well.

Daras: to study

Pronouns	Prefix	Verb: Study Daras
Ana	Bi-	Bidros
Enta	Bti-	Btidros
Ente	Bte-	Btederse
Howwe	Bi	Biedros/Byedros
Hiyye	Bti-	Btidros
Ento	Bte---o	Btederso
Ne7na	Mni-	Mnidros
Hinne	Bye---o	Byederso

I study: **Ana bidros** (means I usually study. Might refer to school or learning a new language for instance)

Example:

- ➢ Ente bel jem3a? *(Are you in the university?)*
- ➢ Eh, ana bidros biology.
- ➢ W 5ayyik sho byidros?

5ayye byidros physics w 2i5te btidros timseel. *(acting)*

the imperative

if you're giving a command/order and telling people to do something, you should use the verb in its imperative form.

And verbs in their imperative form should not have the B or M prefix attached.

	Imperative
2inta	Dros
2inte	Drese
2into	Dreso

The Active Participle

The active participle is essentially an adjective which refers to the action of the verb. In many cases, it may also become a noun which is closely related in meaning to the action of the verb.

First of all, the AP can be used as a regular adjective modifying a noun. In such circumstances the AP will take a **sound masculine or feminine plural *if* the noun it modifies is a plural human noun**.

Example:

There are a lot of people living in Beirut: Fi ktir nes seknin b Beirut

Some active participles, when used as adjectives with a verbal meaning, can have present progressive meaning; some will have present tense meaning; some may have future meaning; some will have present perfect meaning. You will have to learn the meaning(s) of each one. **More often than not the meaning will be clear from the context.**

All in all, active participle can express:

- **Verbs of motion and location**
- **The future**
- **Verbs of mental state**
- **Sometimes a past action**

Compound Tenses

Compound tenses are created by following **ken 'to be'** with a perfect or imperfect verb or active participle. The most common combinations are shown in the table below, using the verb **3imil 'to do'** as an example.

Perfect verb	Ken 3imil	He had done
Imperfect verb	Ken ya3mil	He used to do
Continuous participle	Ken 3am ya3mil	He was doing
Future participle	Ken rah ya3mil	He was going to do
Active participle	Ken 3amil	He was doing

Verb Conjugations

To say

	Perfect	Imperfect	Bi-imperfect
Ana	2elet	2ool	B2ool
2inta	2elet	2ool	Bit2ool
2inte	2elte	2oole	Bit2oole
Howwe	2aal	Y2ool	Bi2ool
Hiyye	2aalit	T2ool	Bit2ool
Ento	2elto	T2oolo	Bit2oolo
Hinne	2aalo	Y2oolo	Bi2oolo
Ne7na	2elna	N2ool	Min2ool

Imperative	
2inta	2ool
2inte	2oole
2into	2oolo

Active Participle	
Masculine	2aayil
Feminine	2aayle
Plural	2ayleen

2inta 2elet 2enno ma ba2a t3ida!
You said you wouldn't do it again!

Hinne bi2oolo eno 3anna 72oo2m, bas ma sheyif hal shi!
They say that we have rights, but I don't see that thing!

2into 2oolo eno badkon tinzalo, fa byinzalo kellon
Just say that you want to go down, then everyone goes down

Ne7na 2elna eno badna nroo7 nekol b mat3am
We said that we want to go eat in a restaurant

2ayleen eno jeye 3asfe 3ala libnen
They are saying that a storm is coming to Lebanon

To read

	Perfect	Imperfect	Bi-imperfect
Ana	2reet	2e2ra	Be2ra
2inta	2reet	2e2ra	Bte2ra
2inte	2reete	2e2re	Bte2re
Howwe	2ere	Ye2ra	Bye2ra
Hiyye	2eret	Te2ra	Bte2ra
Ento	2reeto	Te2ro	Bte2ro
Hinne	2eryo	Ye2ro	Bye2ro
Ne7na	2reena	Ne2ra	Mni2ra

	Imperative
2inta	2ra
2inte	2ri
2into	2ro

	Active Participle
Masculine	2ere
Feminine	2erye
Plural	2eryin

Ana mberi7 2reet kteb ktir 7elo
Yesterday I read a really good book

Hiyye bte2ra bel finjen
She reads in the cup

2inta 2ra kotob bel 2ingleeze la tit7assan
Read books in English in order to improve

2erye ktir kotob bel 2anoon!
She read a lot of law books!

Ana be2ra ktir kotob 3an l Self-help
I read a lot of books about Self-help

To buy

	Perfect	Imperfect	Bi-imperfect
Ana	Shtaret	2ishtre	Bishtre
2inta	Shtaret	Tishtre	Btishtre
2inte	Shtarayte	Tishtre	Btishtre
Howwe	Shtara	Yishtre	Byishtre
Hiyye	Shtarit	Teshtre	Tishtre
Ento	Shtarayto	Tishtro	Btishtro
Hinne	Shtaro	Yishtro	Byishtro
Ne7na	Shtarayna	Nishtre	Mnishtre

	Imperative
2inta	Shtere
2inte	Shtere
2into	Shtero

	Active Participle
Masculine	Mishtre
Feminine	Mishtriyye
Plural	mishtriyyin

Howwe shtara 3afesh jdid
He bought new furniture

Ento btishtro bala ma tfakro!
You buy without thinking!

A7la shi enno tishtre bet bel reef
The best thing is to buy a house in the village

L siyesiyye mishtriyyin l bnooke kellon
The politicians have bought all the banks

Shtere firsheyit snen jdide
Buy a new toothbrush

To visit

	Perfect	Imperfect	Bi-imperfect
Ana	Zeret	Zoor	Bzoor
2inta	Zeret	Tzoor	Bitzoor
2inte	Zirte	Tzoore	Bitzoore
Howwe	Zaar	Yzoor	Bizoor
Hiyye	Zaarit	Tzoor	Bitzoor
Ento	Zerto	Tzooro	bitzooro
Hinne	Zaaro	Yzooro	Bizooro
Ne7na	Zerna	Nzoor	Minzoor

	Imperative
2inta	Zoor
2inte	Zoore
2into	Zooro

	Active Participle
Masculine	Zeyir
Feminine	Zeyra
Plural	Zeyrin

Ana zeret ktir bilden b 7ayete
I visited alot of countries in my life

Bitzoore sittik w jiddik 2aw2at?
Do you visit your grandma and grandpa sometimes?

Tzooro mgharit j3ita?
Shall we visit Jeita Grotto?

Zoorne 3ande bel bet
Visit me at my home

Eh kelna zeyrin shi balad tene
Yea we all visited another country

To go

	Perfect	Imperfect	Bi-imperfect
Ana	Re7et	Roo7	Broo7
2inta	Re7et	Troo7	Bitroo7
2inte	Ri7te	Troo7e	Bitroo7e
Howwe	Raa7	Yroo7	Biroo7
Hiyye	Raa7it	Troo7	Bitroo7
Ento	Re7to	Troo7o	Bitroo7o
Hinne	Raa7o	Yroo7o	Biroo7o
Ne7na	Re7na	Nroo7	Minroo7

Imperative	
2inta	Roo7
2inte	Roo7e
2into	Roo7o

Active Participle	
Masculine	Rayi7
Feminine	Ray7a
Plural	Ray7in

Ana re7et abel b marra 3ala Canada
I went before to Canada

Troo7 t2addim shakwa eza badda
She can go file a complaint if she wants to

Troo7o bokra nekol sushi?
Wanna go tomorrow eat sushi?

Ray7in bokra 3ala trablos
We are going tomorrow to Tripoli

Eza ken l mat3am msakkar, minroo7 3ala mat3am ghayro
If the restaurant was closed we`ll just go to another restaurant

To try

	Perfect	Imperfect	Bi-imperfect
Ana	7awalet	7awel	B7awel
2inta	7awalet	T7awel	Bit7awel
2inte	7awalte	T7awle	Bit7awle
Howwe	7awal	Y7awil	Bi7awil
Hiyye	7awalit	T7awil	Bit7awil
Ento	7awalto	T7awlo	Bit7awlo
Hinne	7awalo	Y7awlo	Bi7awlo
Ne7na	7awalna	N7awil	Min7awil

	Imperative
2inta	7awil
2inte	7awle
2into	7awlo

	Active Participle
Masculine	M7awil
Feminine	M7awle
Plural	M7awlin

Ana b7awil 2i7ke 3arabe bas sa3be l logha
I try to speak Arabic but the language is hard

T7awle nisbo2 l seyara lle 7adna?
Shall we try to race the car next to us?

7awalna nimro2 b Jal El Dib bas fi 3aj2it ser 2awiyye
We tried to pass through Jal El Dib but there`s traffic

7awil teje bokra 3amlin kousa
Try to come by tomorrow we are making Zucchinis

Tol3it m7awle ta3mil hacking bas ma zabtit ma3a
It appears she has tried to hack but it didn`t work out

To come

	Perfect	Imperfect	Bi-imperfect
Ana	Jeet	2eje	Beje
2inta	Jeet	Teje	Bteje
2inte	Jeete	Teje	Bteje
Howwe	2eja	Yeje	Byeje
Hiyye	2ejit	Teje	Bteje
Ento	Jeeto	Tejo	Btejo
Hinne	2ejo	Yejo	Byejo
Ne7na	Jina	Neje	Mneje

	Imperative
2inta	Ta3a
2inte	Ta3e
2into	Ta3o

	Active Participle
Masculine	Jey
Feminine	Jeye
Plural	Jeyin

Teje nroo7 3ala mat3am?
Let`s go to a restaurant

Jina kelna sawa 3ala l se7a
We came altogether to the field

Ta3a la 3ande 3al 5amse
Come to me at five

Howwe ken jeye 3al sitte bas 3emel 7adis
He wanted to come at 3 but made an accident

Btejo la 3ande lyum?
Will you come to my place today?

To open

	Perfect	Imperfect	Bi-imperfect
Ana	Fata7it	2ifta7	Bifta7
2inta	Fata7it	Tifta7	Btifta7
2inte	Fata7te	Tifta7e	Btifta7e
Howwe	Fata7	Yifta7	Byifta7
Hiyye	Fata7it	Tifta7	Btifta7
Ento	Fata7to	Tifta7o	Btifta7o
Hinne	Fata7o	Yifta7o	Byifta7o
Ne7na	Fata7na	Nifta7	Mnifta7

	Imperative
2inta	Ftaa7
2inte	Fta7e
2into	Fta7o

	Active Participle
Masculine	Feti7
Feminine	Fet7a
Plural	Fet7in

Fata7te 2anninet Pepsi mberi7 shi?
Did you open Pepsi bottle yesterday?

Byifta7o kel yom 2anninet beera
They open everyday a beer bottle

L bnooke byifta7o kil l nhar
The banks open all day

Ftaa7 l beb ana seret wasil
Open the door I am almost there

2awlak ba3da fet7a l supermarket?
Do you think the supermarket is still open?

To help

	Perfect	Imperfect	Bi-imperfect
Ana	Se3adit	Se3id	Bse3id
2inta	Se3adit	Tse3id	Bitse3id
2inte	Se3adte	Tse3de	Bitse3de
Howwe	Se3ad	Yse3id	Bise3id
Hiyye	Se3adit	Tse3id	Bitse3id
Ento	Se3adto	Tse3do	Bitse3do
Hinne	Se3ado	Yse3do	Bise3do
Ne7na	Se3adna	Nse3id	Minse3id

	Imperative
2inta	Se3id
2inte	Se3de
2into	Se3do

	Active Participle
Masculine	Mse3id
Feminine	Mse3de
Plural	Mse3din

Ana se3adit taffe l 7aree2 lamma sar fi 7aree2a
I helped put out the fire when one broke out

Ahamma shi eno yinzal yse3id
The most important thing is to go down and help

Bitse3id ahlak bel bet?
Do you help your parents at home?

2oum se3id 2emmak
Go help your mother

Lezim kelna nse3id rif2atna
We should all help our friends

To hope

	Perfect	Imperfect	Bi-imperfect
Ana	Tmannet	Tmanna	Bitmanna
2inta	Tmannet	Titmanna	Btitmanna
2inte	Tmannayte	Titmanne	Btitmanne
Howwe	Tmanna	Yitmanna	Byitmanna
Hiyye	Tmannit	Titmanna	Btitmanna
Ento	Tmannayto	Titmanno	Btitmanno
Hinne	Tmanno	Yitmanno	Byitmanno
Ne7na	Tmannayna	Nitmanna	Mnitmanna

	Imperative
2inta	Tmanna
2inte	Tmanne
2into	Tmanno

	Active Participle
Masculine	Mitmanne
Feminine	Mitmanniye
Plural	Mitmanniyin

Ana bitmanna eno ybattil fi 7roob bel 3alam
I hope that there would be no wars in the world

Tmanne eno tinja7e bel 2imti7an
I hope that you will succeed in the exam

Tmannayna eno neje 3a libnen hal sene bas ma 2deret
We hoped to come to Lebanon this year but we couldn't

Lezim yitmanno la yit7a22a2 2omniyeton
They should hope for their wishes to come true

Ana bitmanna eno tinja7 l sawra
I hope/wish that the revolution will win

To learn

	Perfect	Imperfect	Bi-imperfect
Ana	T3allamet	2it3allam	Bit3allam
2inta	T3allamet	Tit3allam	Btit3allam
2inte	T3allamte	Tit3allame	Btit3allame
Howwe	T3allam	Yit3allam	Byit3allam
Hiyye	T3allamet	Tit3allam	Btit3allam
Ento	T3allamto	Tit3allamo	Btit3allamo
Hinne	T3allamo	Yit3allamo	Byit3allamo
Ne7na	T3allamna	Nit3allam	Mnit3allam

Imperative	
2inta	T3allam
2inte	T3allame
2into	T3allamo

	Active Participle
Masculine	Mit3alam
Feminine	Mit3alme
Plural	Mit3almin

Ana t3allamet eno 3layye 72oo2 w wejbet
I learned that I have rights and duties

2aw2at l sheri3 bi3allim aktar min l madrase
Sometimes the street teaches more than the school

T3allam la tinja7 bel 7ayet
Learn to succeed in life

Howwe sha5es 2edame w mit3allim
He's a good and educated guy

5alleya toghlat, hek btit3allam
Let her make mistakes, that's how she learns

To play

	Perfect	Imperfect	Bi-imperfect
Ana	L3ebet	2il3ab	Bil3ab
2inta	L3ebet	Til3ab	Btil3ab
2inte	L3ebte	Til3abe	Btil3abe
Howwe	Le3eb	Yil3ab	Byil3ab
Hiyye	Le3bit	Til3ab	Btil3ab
Ento	L3ebto	Til3abo	Btil3abo
Hinne	Le3bo	Yil3abo	Byil3abo
Ne7na	L3ebna	Nil3ab	Mnil3ab

	Imperative
2inta	L3ab
2inte	L3abe
2into	L3abo

	Active Participle
Masculine	Le3ib
Feminine	Le3be
Plural	Le3bin

Til3abe Maro kart?
Shall we play Mario kart?

L3ebto hal li3be abel b marra?
Did you play this game before?

L3ab gher li3be 3laye!
Play another game on me! (Don't trick me)

Hay kella le3be w ne7na mish fahmenin
This is all a game and we don't understand

Ntor la yeje Jad la nil3ab kelna sawa
Wait till Jad comes for us to play together

To return

	Perfect	Imperfect	Bi-imperfect
Ana	Rje3et	2irja3	Birja3
2inta	Rje3et	Tirja3	Btirja3
2inte	Rji3te	Tirja3e	Btirja3e
Howwe	Reje3	Yirja3	Byirja3
Hiyye	Rej3it	Tirja3	Btirja3
Ento	Rje3to	Tirja3o	Btirja3o
Hinne	Rej3o	Yirja3o	Byirja3o
Ne7na	Rje3na	Nirja3	Mnirja3

	Imperative
2inta	Rja3
2inte	Rja3e
2into	Rja3o

	Active Participle
Masculine	Reji3
Feminine	Rej3a
Plural	Rej3in

Libnan ra7 yirja3
Lebanon will return

Rja3 la hon w lim l li3be!
Return here and pick up the toy!

Yalla ana rayi7 bas reji3 ba3ed shway
I am going but I'm return in a bit

Rja3o kelkon la hon bser3a!
Return back here all of you now!

Kil l masare l masrou2a ra7 tirja3
All of the stolen money will return

To become

	Perfect	Imperfect	Bi-imperfect
Ana	Seret	Seer	Bseer
2inta	Seret	Tseer	Bitseer
2inte	Serte	Tseere	Bitseere
Howwe	Sar	Yseer	Biseer
Hiyye	Sarit	Tseer	Bitseer
Ento	Serto	Tseero	Bitseero
Hinne	Saro	Yseero	Biseero
Ne7na	Serna	Nseer	Minseer

	Imperative
2inta	Seer
2inte	Seere
2into	Seero

	Active Participle
Masculine	Sayir
Feminine	Sayra
Plural	Sayrin

Ana seret fa2eer
I became poor

2inta lezim tseer ya 7akeem ya mhandis
You must become either doctor or engineer

Eza tarakto l tab5a 3al nar bitseer sawda
If you leave the food on the stove it will become black

Lezim ne7na nseer minfit7in aktar
We must become more open

2inte sayra mitle
You have become like me

To stop

	Perfect	Imperfect	Bi-imperfect
Ana	Wa22afit	Wa22if	Bwa22if
2inta	Wa22afit	Twa22if	Bitwa22if
2inte	Wa22afte	Twa2fe	Bitwa2fe
Howwe	Wa22af	Ywa22if	Biwa22if
Hiyye	Wa22afit	Twa22if	Bitwa22if
Ento	Wa22afto	Twa2fo	Bitwa2fo
Hinne	Wa22afo	Ywa2fo	Biwa2fo
Ne7na	Wa22afna	Nwa22if	Minwa22if

Imperative	
2inta	Wa22if
2inte	Wa2fe
2into	Wa2fo

Active Participle	
Masculine	Mwa22if
Feminine	Mwa2fe
Plural	Mwa2fin

Ana wa22afit e5od dawa
I stopped taking the medicine

Eza bit2ool kilme, biwa2fo yreddo 3lek
If you say a word, they will stop replying

Lezim nwa22if nekol ktir bel lel
We should stop eating a lot at night

Please wa2fo tde2oule bel lel
Please stop calling me at night

Bas twa2fo ento minwa22if ne7na
When you stop then we'll stop

To sleep

	Perfect	Imperfect	Bi-imperfect
Ana	Nemet	Nem	Bnem
2inta	Nemet	Tnem	Bitnem
2inte	Nimte	Tneme	Bitneme
Howwe	Nem	Ynem	Binem
Hiyye	Nemit	Tnem	Bitnem
Ento	Nemto	Tnemo	Bitnemo
Hinne	Nemo	Ynemo	Binemo
Ne7na	Nemna	Nnem	Minnem

	Imperative
2inta	Nem
2inte	Neme
2into	Nemo

	Active Participle
Masculine	Neyim
Feminine	Neyme
Plural	Neymin

Ana nemet mberi7 l se3a tis3a bel lel
Yesterday I slept at nice at night

Howwe ma binem 2ella ma ykoon fi mosee2a
He doesn't sleep until there's music

Minnem kelna b 2ouda we7de
We all sleep in one room

Ma fik ti7ke ma3o halla2 la2anno neyim. Di2 ba3den
You can't talk to him now cause he's sleeping. Call later

Neme bakkir la tfee2e bakkir
Sleep early to wake up early

To fall

	Perfect	Imperfect	Bi-imperfect
Ana	W2e3et	2ou2a3	Bou2a3
2inta	W2e3et	Tou2a3	Btou2a3
2inte	W2i3te	Tou2a3e	Btou2a3e
Howwe	We2e3	You2a3	Byou2a3
Hiyye	We23it	Tou2a3	Btou2a3
Ento	W2e3to	Tou2a3o	Btou2a3o
Hinne	We23o	You2a3o	Byou2a3o
Ne7na	W2e3na	Nou2a3	Mnou2a3

Imperative	
2inta	W2aa3
2inte	W2a3e
2into	W2a3o

Active Participle	
Masculine	We2i3
Feminine	We23a
Plural	We23in

W2e3et bel fa5
You fell into the trap

Ntibhe tou2a3e bel joura
Watch out not to fall in the hole

Lezim you2a3o kellon la yimshe 7alna
They all have to fall to work out for us

W2aa3 bas hiyye tshoufak
Fall down when she sees you

Ana we2i3 bel 7ob 3al 2e5ir
I have fallen in love to the most

To watch

	Perfect	Imperfect	Bi-imperfect
Ana	7deret	2i7dar	Bi7dar
2inta	7deret	Ti7dar	Bti7dare
2inte	7dirte	Ti7dare	Bti7dare
Howwe	7eder	Yi7dar	Byi7dar
Hiyye	7idrit	Ti7dar	Bti7dar
Ento	7derto	Ti7daro	Bti7daro
Hinne	7edro	Yi7daro	Byi7daro
Ne7na	7derna	Ni7dar	Mni7dar

	Imperative
2inta	7daar
2inte	7dare
2into	7daro

	Active Participle
Masculine	7aadir
Feminine	7aadra
Plural	7aadrin

Ana bi7dar kel yom 2a5baar
I watch the news daily

7dirte mberi7 l 7al2a l jdide?
Did you watch yesterday the new episode?

Bti7daro Friends 3al Netflix?
Do you watch Friends on Netflix?

7daar mosalsal ghayro wlo
Watch another series come on

7aadrin mosalsal Game of Thrones?
Have you watched Game of Thrones?

To eat

	Perfect	Imperfect	Bi-imperfect
Ana	2akalet	2ekol	Bekol
2inta	2akalet	Tekol	Btekol
2inte	2akalte	Tekle	Btekle
Howwe	2akal	Yekol	Byekol
Hiyye	2akalet	Tekol	Btekol
Ento	2akalto	Teklo	Bteklo
Hinne	2akalo	Yeklo	Byeklo
Ne7na	2akalna	Nekol	Mnekol

	Imperative
2inta	Kol
2inte	Kele
2into	Kelo

	Active Participle
Masculine	Mekil
Feminine	Mekle
Plural	Meklin

Ana bekol terwi2a kel yom
I eat breakfast everyday

Ya ret law 2akalto mberi7 ma3na
I hoped you ate with us

Kele shorba kel yom la tso77e
Eat soup everyday to get better

Mekil kousa me7she abel?
Have you eaten stuffed zucchinis before?

2imshe nroo7 nekol b mat3am
Let's go eat in a restaurant

To know

	Perfect	Imperfect	Bi-imperfect
Ana	3refet	2a3rif	Ba3rif
2inta	3refet	Ta3rif	Bta3rif
2inte	3rifte	Ta3erfe	Bta3irfe
Howwe	3eref	Ya3rif	Bya3rif
Hiyye	3erfit	Ta3rif	Bta3rif
Ento	3refto	Ta3erfo	Bta3erfo
Hinne	3erfo	Ya3erfo	Bya3erfo
Ne7na	3refna	Na3rif	Mna3rif

	Imperative
2inta	3raaf
2inte	3rafe
2into	3rafo

	Active Participle
Masculine	3aarif
Feminine	3aarfe
Plural	3aarfin

3rfite eno Shadi sa2at bel 2imti7an?
Did you know that Shadi failed the exam?

Kelna mna3rif eno hayda l shi mish mazboot
We all know that this thing is not correct

Lezim ta3erfo eno hayda l shi sar
You have to know that this thing happened

3raaf eno bokra lezim kelna nitla3
Know that tomorrow we all have to go

Ana mish 3aarif eza bokra 3otle aw la2
I don't know if tomorrow is holiday or not

To wait

	Perfect	Imperfect	Bi-imperfect
Ana	Natarit	2ontor	Bontor
2inta	Natarit	Tintor	Btintor
2inte	Natarte	Tontre	Btontre
Howwe	Natar	Yontor	Byontor
Hiyye	Natarit	Tontor	Btontor
Ento	Natarto	Tontro	Btontro
Hinne	Nataro	Yontro	Byontro
Ne7na	Natarna	Nontor	Mnontor

	Imperative
2inta	Ntor
2inte	Ntore
2into	Ntoro

	Active Participle
Masculine	Naatir
Feminine	Naatra
Plural	Naatreen

Akrah 3layye 2ontor bel dor
I hate to wait in line

2inte natarte ktir la jeet ana
You waited a lot till I came

Ento 3adatan btontro ktir lal akel?
Do you usually wait a long time for the food?

Ntor la 2eje ana
Wait till I come

La 2ayemta ra7 dal natra?
Till when will I keep on waiting?

To wash

	Perfect	Imperfect	Bi-imperfect
Ana	Ghassalet	Ghassil	Bghassil
2inta	Ghassalet	Tghassil	Bitghassil
2inte	Ghassalte	Tghassle	Bitghassle
Howwe	Ghassal	Yghassil	Bighassil
Hiyye	Ghassalit	Tghassil	Bitghassil
Ento	Ghassalto	Tghasslo	Bitghasslo
Hinne	Ghassalo	Yghasslo	Bighasslo
Ne7na	Ghassalna	Nghassil	Minghassil

	Imperative
2inta	Ghassil
2inte	Ghassle
2into	Ghasslo

	Active Participle
Masculine	Mghassil
Feminine	Mghassle
Plural	Mghassleen

Ghassle 2idayke abel ma tekle
Wash your hands before you eat

Lezim tghassil l tiffe7a abel ma tekela
You should wash the apple before you eat it

Ana bghassil jisme kel yom
I wash my body everyday

Ouf, ben mghassil seyyartak!
Wow, it looks like you washed your car!

Kellon ghassalo seyyaraton abel ma yejo
They all washed their cars before they came

To live

	Perfect	Imperfect	Bi-imperfect
Ana	Sakanit	2iskon	Biskon
2inta	Sakanit	Tiskon	Btiskon
2inte	Sakante	Tesekne	Btesekne
Howwe	Sakan	Yiskon	Byiskon
Hiyye	Sakanit	Tiskon	Btiskon
Ento	Sakanto	Tesekno	Btesekno
Hinne	Sakano	Yesekno	Byesekno
Ne7na	Sakanna	Niskon	Mniskon

Imperative	
2inta	Skon
2inte	Skene
2into	Skeno

Active Participle	
Masculine	Sekin
Feminine	Sekne
Plural	Seknin

Ana sakanit b 2oroppa sneen
I lived in Europe for years

Eza baddik fike tesekne 3ande kam shaher la tle2e bet 2elik
If you want, you can live by my place a couple of months till you find a home

L 3asfoor byiskon 3al shajra
The bird lives on the tree

Ta3o niskon kelna sawa b bet wa7ad
Let's all of us live together

Skon 3ande eza badak
Live with me if you want to

Ana sekin b Beirut
I live in Beirut

To ask

	Perfect	Imperfect	Bi-imperfect
Ana	Sa2alet	2is2al	Bis2al
2inta	Sa2alet	Tis2al	Btis2al
2inte	Sa2alte	Tis2ale	Btis2ale
Howwe	Sa2al	Yis2al	Byis2al
Hiyye	Sa2alit	Tis2al	Btis2al
Ento	Sa2alto	Tis2alo	Btis2alo
Hinne	Sa2alo	Yis2alo	Byis2alo
Ne7na	Sa2alna	Nis2al	Mnis2al

	Imperative
2inta	S2aal
2inte	S2ale
2into	S2alo

	Active Participle
Masculine	Se2il
Feminine	Se2le
Plural	Se2lin

Sa2alet ahlak sho 3amlin akel lyum?
Did you ask your parents what did they cook today?

Hiyye lezim tis2al ayemta 7a yin3amalo l 2imti7anet
She has to ask when will the exams take place

Ne7na 3atool mnis2al sho 3am b seer
We always ask what is going on

S2aal la ta3rif
Ask to know

Hiyye kenit se2le abel bas ma 2ijeha jaweb
She has had asked before but she didn't get an answer

To write

	Perfect	Imperfect	Bi-imperfect
Ana	Katabit	2iktob	Biktob
2inta	Katabit	Tiktob	Btiktob
2inte	Katabte	Teketbe	Bteketbe
Howwe	Katab	Yiktob	Byiktob
Hiyye	Katabit	Tiktob	Btiktob
Ento	Katabto	Teketbo	Bteketbo
Hinne	Katabo	Yeketbo	Byeketbo
Ne7na	Katabna	Niktob	Mniktob

Imperative	
2inta	Ktob
2inte	Ktebe
2into	ktebo

Active Participle	
Masculine	Ketib
Feminine	Ketbe
Plural	Ketbin

Ana halla2 3am biktob hal kteb
I am now writing this book

Howwe lezim yiktob kel shi bifakkir fi
He must write down everything he thinks of

Hiyye btiktob b daftara kel yom
She writes in her notebook everyday

Ktebo l 2ajwebe 3ala war2it l 2ajwebe
Write the answers on the answers paper

Hiyye sarit ketbe kteben
She has written two books

To finish

	Perfect	Imperfect	Bi-imperfect
Ana	5allasit	5allis	B5allis
2inta	5allasit	T5allis	Bit5allis
2inte	5allaste	T5allse	Bit5allse
Howwe	5allas	Y5allis	Bi5allis
Hiyye	5allasit	T5allis	Bit5allis
Ento	5allasto	T5allso	Bit5allso
Hinne	5allaso	Y5allso	Bi5allso
Ne7na	5allasna	N5allis	Min5allis

	Imperative
2inta	5allis
2inte	5allse
2into	5allso

	Active Participle
Masculine	M5allis
Feminine	M5allse
Plural	M5allsin

Ana lezim 5allis b 2asra3 wa2et
I have to finish as fast as possible

Howwe 5allas w hayye sar jeye
He finished and is on his way

Hiyye 3adatan bit5allis 3al se3a 5amse
She usually finished at five o'clock

Yalla 5allis ta3a ana zah2an
Finish and come I'm bored

Tol3o m5alsin min zamen w ma 2aloolna
They appear to have already finished but didn't tell us

To begin

	Perfect	Imperfect	Bi-imperfect
Ana	Ballashit	Ballish	Bballish
2inta	Ballashit	Tballish	Bitballish
2inte	Ballashte	Tballshe	Bitballshe
Howwe	Ballash	Yballish	Biballish
Hiyye	Ballashit	Tballish	Bitballish
Ento	Ballashto	Tballsho	Bitballsho
Hinne	Ballasho	Yballsho	Bibalsho
Ne7na	Ballashna	Nballish	Minballish

Imperative	
2inta	Ballish
2inte	Ballshe
2into	Ballsho

Active Participle	
Masculine	Mballish
Feminine	Mballshe
Plural	Mballshin

Ana ra7 ballish sheghel min bokra
I will begin work from tomorrow

Ballashte tsou2e 2aw 5ayfene
Did you begin driving or still scared?

3adatan l mosalsal biballish 3al tlete
Normally the series begins at three

Ballsho tishteghlo mni7 la nousa2 fikon
Start working well to trust you

L 2ossa mballshe min zamen
The story began a long time ago

To wear

	Perfect	Imperfect	Bi-imperfect
Ana	Lbeset	2ilbos	Bilbos
2inta	Lbeset	Tilbos	Btilbos
2inte	Lbiste	Telebse	Btelebse
Howwe	Lebes	Yilbos	Byilbos
Hiyye	Libsit	Tilbos	Btilbos
Ento	Lbesto	Telebso	Btelebso
Hinne	Lebso	Yelebso	Byelebso
Ne7na	Lbesna	Nilbos	Mnilbos

	Imperative
2inta	Lbos
2inte	Lbese
2into	Lbeso

	Active Participle
Masculine	Lebis
Feminine	Lebse
Plural	Lebsin

Yalla 3am bilbos
I am wearing

Kil l tlemiz lezim yelebso maryool
All of the students must wear a costume

Kelna lbesna a7mar minshen 3id l 2isti2lel
We all wore red for the independence day

Lbese bser3a w l7a2ine
Wear quick and follow me

Sho lebis?
What are you wearing?

To sell

	Perfect	Imperfect	Bi-imperfect
Ana	Be3et	Bi3	Bbi3
2inta	Be3et	Tbi3	Bitbi3
2inte	Bi3te	Tbee3e	Bitbee3e
Howwe	Be3	Ybee3	Bibee3
Hiyye	Be3it	Tbee3	Bitbee3
Ento	Be3to	Tbee3o	Bitbee3o
Hinne	Be3o	Ybee3o	Bibee3o
Ne7na	Be3na	Nbee3	Minbee3

Imperative	
2inta	Bee3
2inte	Bee3e
2into	Bee3o

Active Participle	
Masculine	Beyi3
Feminine	Bey3a
Plural	Bey3in

Ana bbi3 3aranees b Beirut
I sell corn in Beirut

Howwe lezim ybee3 kel yom la yi2dar yidfa3 l 2ajaar
He has to sell everyday in order to be able to pay rent

Hiyye be3it nos 3afesh bayta
She sold half of her house's furniture

Bee3 kel shi 3andak ye w ta3a
Sell everything you have and then come

Saro bey3in shi 5amseen 3ilbit baskot
They have sold around fifty cookie boxes

To forget

	Perfect	Imperfect	Bi-imperfect
Ana	Nseet	2insa	Binsa
2inta	Nseet	Tinsa	Btinsa
2inte	Nseete	Tinse	Nseete
Howwe	Nese	Yinsa	Byinsa
Hiyye	Nisyit	Tinsa	Btinsa
Ento	Nesyo	Tinso	Btinso
Hinne	Nesyo	Yinso	Byinso
Ne7na	Nseena	Ninsa	Mninsa

Imperative	
2inta	2insa
2inte	2inse
2into	2inso

Active Participle	
Masculine	Nese
Feminine	Nesye
Plural	Nesyin

2inta sayer btinsa ktir
You are forgetting a lot

Hiyye nisyit tjib ma3a l charger
She forgot to bring the charger with her

Ma ken lezim tinso hal shaghle!
You weren't supposed to forget this thing!

2inse lle sar, mish mistehle l 2ossa!
Forget what happened, it doesn't need that much!

Shaklo nese eno lyom 3anna maw3ad
He seems to have forgot that we have a meeting today

To stay

	Perfect	Imperfect	Bi-imperfect
Ana	Dallet	Dal	Bdal
2inta	Dallet	Tdal	Bitdal
2inte	Dallayte	Tdalle	Bitdalle
Howwe	Dal	Ydal	Bidal
Hiyye	Dallit	Tdal	Bitdal
Ento	Dallayto	Tdalo	Bitdallo
Hinne	Dallo	Ydallo	Bidallo
Ne7na	Dallayna	Ndal	Mindal

	Imperative
2inta	Dal
2inte	Dalle
2into	Dallo

	Active Participle
Masculine	Dalil (Be2e)
Feminine	Dalle (Be2ye)
Plural	Dallin (Be2yin)

* The original active participle form is not commonly used

Ana ra7 dal hon la bokra
I will stay here till tomorrow

2inte dallayte hon ma3 2enno 5olis dawem l 3amal!
You stayed here even though work time is over!

Hinne lezim ydallo hon w ma yfello
They shall stay here and not leave!

Ente dal hon la roo7 ana jib l akel
You stay here till I get the food

Ne7na be2yin hon w mish fellin
We are staying here and not leaving

To speak

	Perfect	Imperfect	Bi-imperfect
Ana	7kit	2i7ke	Bi7ke
2inta	7kit	Ti7ke	Bti7ke
2inte	7kite	Ti7ke	Bti7ke
Howwe	7eke	Yi7ke	Byi7ke
Hiyye	7ikyit	Ti7ke	Bti7ke
Ento	7keeto	Ti7ko	Bti7ko
Hinne	7ikyo	Yi7ko	Byi7ko
Ne7na	7kina	Ni7ke	Mni7ke

Imperative	
2inta	2i7ke
2inte	2i7ke
2into	2i7ko

Active Participle	
Masculine	7eke
Feminine	7ekye
Plural	7ekyin

2inte lezim ti7ke ma3 l modeer!
You have to speak to the manager!

Hiyye bti7ke ktir
She speaks a lot

Ento 7keeto kel l wa2et, fine 2i7ke ana halla2?
You spoke the whole time, can I speak now?

Yalla 2i7ke la shoof
Talk, let's see

Hinne tol3o 7ekyin 3le 3ashen hek mit5an2een
They have talked about him that's why they had a fight

To give

	Perfect	Imperfect	Bi-imperfect
Ana	3atet	2a3te	Ba3te
2inta	3atet	Ta3te	Bta3te
2inte	3atayte	Ta3te	Bta3te
Howwe	3ata	Ya3te	Bya3te
Hiyye	3atet	Ta3te	Bta3te
Ento	3atayto	Ta3to	Bta3to
Hinne	3ato	Ya3to	Bya3to
Ne7na	3atayna	Na3te	Mna3te

	Imperative
2inta	3ti
2inte	3ti
2into	3to

	Active Participle
Masculine	3ati
Feminine	3atye
Plural	3atyin

2inta lezim ta3te kill le 3andak bel sheghel
You have to give everything you have in the job

Hiyye 3atet 2alam la Shadi
She gave a pen to Shadi

Ne7na mna3te droos kel yom
We give lessons every day

3tine masare
Give me money

Hiyye 3atye kel shi la wleda
She has given everything to her kids

To cook

	Perfect	Imperfect	Bi-imperfect
Ana	Taba5et	2otbo5	Botbo5
2inta	Taba5et	Titbo5	Btitbo5
2inte	Taba5te	Totob5e	Btotob5e
Howwe	Taba5	Yitbo5	Byitbo5
Hiyye	Taba5et	Titbo5	Btitbo5
Ento	Taba5to	Totob5o	Btotob5o
Hinne	Taba5o	Yotob5o	Byotob5o
Ne7na	Taba5na	Notbo5	Mnotbo5

Imperative	
2inta	Tbo5
2inte	Tbo5e
2into	Tbo5o

Active Participle	
Masculine	Taabi5
Feminine	Taab5a
Plural	Taab5in

Ana lezim 2otbo5 lyum sarle yawmen 3am bekol akel min barra
I have to cook today; I have been ordering food for the last 2 days

Howwe taba5 la 2emmo w bayyo lamma keno maridin
He cooked for his mom and dad when they were sick

Ento btotob5o bas la 2elkon aw kamen lal kil?
Do you cook only for yourselves or also for everyone?

Yalla tbo5 seret wasil
Cook I'm almost there

Hiyye taab5a ma3karona
She has cooked spaghetti

To rest

	Perfect	Imperfect	Bi-imperfect
Ana	Rte7et	2irte7	Birte7
2inta	Rte7et	Tirte7	Btirte7
2inte	Rti7te	Tirte7e	Btirte7e
Howwe	Rte7	Yirte7	Byirte7
Hiyye	Rte7it	Tirte7	Btirte7
Ento	Rte7to	Tirte7o	Btirte7o
Hinne	Rte7o	Yirte7o	Byirte7o
Ne7na	Rte7na	Nirte7	Mnirte7

	Imperative
2inta	Rte7
2inte	Rte7e
2into	Rte7o

	Active Participle
Masculine	Mirte7
Feminine	Mirte7a
Plural	Mirte7in

Ana lezim 2itsatta7 w 2irte7 shway
I have to lay down and rest a little

Btirte7e eza 3taytik masare?
Will you rest if I gave you money?

Hinne rte7o min zamen
They rested a long time ago

Rte7o ento, ana broo7 bjib ghrad
Rest, I'll go get groceries

Shaklik mirte7a ktir 3al ta5et
You seem rested a lot on the bed

To study

	Perfect	Imperfect	Bi-imperfect
Ana	Darasit	2idros	Btidros
2inta	Darasit	Tidros	Btidros
2inte	Daraste	Tederse	Btederse
Howwe	Daras	Yidros	Byidros
Hiyye	Darasit	Tidros	Btidros
Ento	Darasto	Tederso	Btederso
Hinne	Daraso	Yederso	Byederso
Ne7na	Darasna	Nidros	Mnidros

	Imperative
2inta	Dros
2inte	Drese
2into	Dreso

	Active Participle
Masculine	Deris
Feminine	Derse
Plural	Dersin

Eza btederse, btinja7e
If you study, you pass

Hiyye darasit ktir bas ma naja7it
She studied a lot but didn't pass

Ne7na lezim 3atool nidros
We must always study

2oum dros bokra fi 2imti7an
Go study you have a test tomorrow

Deris?
Have you studied?

To think

	Perfect	Imperfect	Bi-imperfect
Ana	Fakkarit	Fakkir	Bfakkir
2inta	Fakkarit	Tfakkir	Bitfakkir
2inte	Fakkarte	Tfakre	Bitfakre
Howwe	Fakkar	Yfakkir	Bifakkir
Hiyye	Fakkarit	Tfakkir	Bitfakkir
Ento	Fakkarto	Tfakro	Bitfakro
Hinne	Fakkaro	Yfakro	Bifakro
Ne7na	Fakkarna	Nfakkir	Minfakkir

	Imperative
2inta	Fakkir
2inte	Fakre
2into	Fakro

	Active Participle
Masculine	Mfakkir
Feminine	Mfakre
Plural	Mfakrin

3am fakkir roo7 ekol b mat3am
I'm thinking on going to eat in a restaurant

Howwe fakkar eno ken lezim yde2 abel ma yeje
He though he should've called before coming

Hinne bifakro enno hinne 3atool ma3on 7a2
They think that they are always correct

Fakkir 2abel ma ti7ke
Think before you talk

Keno mfakrin eno l maw3ad lyom
They have though that the appointment is today

To move

	Perfect	Imperfect	Bi-imperfect
Ana	7arrakit	7arrik	B7arrik
2inta	7arrakit	T7arrik	Bit7arrik
2inte	7arrakte	T7arrke	Bit7arrke
Howwe	7arrak	Y7arrik	Bi7arrik
Hiyye	7arrakit	T7arrik	Bit7arrik
Ento	7arrakto	T7arrko	Bit7arko
Hinne	7arrako	Y7arrko	Bi7arko
Ne7na	7arrakna	N7arrik	Min7arrik

	Imperative
2inta	7arrik
2inte	7arke
2into	7arko

	Active Participle
Masculine	M7arrik
Feminine	M7arke
Plural	M7arkin

L 7akeem 2al lezim t7arke 2idik 3atool
The doctor said that you should always move your hand

Ento 7arrakto shi ma7al l sofa?
Did you move the sofa?

Hay li3be kellon y7arko ijron sawa
That's a game to move their feet together

7arrik 7alak w jible 2anninet may
Move yourself and get a bottle of water

Tol3o m7arkin l ma7al w ma 2eylinle!
They have moved the place and didn't tell me!

To throw

	Perfect	Imperfect	Bi-imperfect
Ana	Kabbet	Kib	Bkib
2inta	Kabbet	Tkib	Bitkib
2inte	kabbayte	Tkibbe	Bitkibbe
Howwe	Kab	Ykib	Bikib
Hiyye	Kabbit	Tkib	Bitkib
Ento	Kabbayto	Tkebbo	Bitkebbo
Hinne	Kabbo	Ykebbo	Bikebbo
Ne7na	Kabbayna	Nkib	Minkib

	Imperative
2inta	Kib
2inte	Kibbe
2into	Kibbo

	Active Participle
Masculine	Kebib
Feminine	Kebbe
Plural	kebbin

Ana kel yom bkib l zbele
I throw the trash out everyday

Howwe kab se3to bel may!
He threw his watch in the water!

Ne7na ma lezim nkib zbele bel ba7er!
We must not throw trash in the sea!

Kibbile l 2alam
Throw me the pen

Ma ba3rif le kebbin 7alon hal kabbe
I don't know why they threw themselves like this

To sit

	Perfect	Imperfect	Bi-imperfect
Ana	2a3adet	2i23od	Bi23od
2inta	2a3adet	Ti23od	Bti23od
2inte	2a3adte	Te2e3de	Bte2e3de
Howwe	2a3ad	Yi23od	Byi23od
Hiyye	2a3adit	Ti23od	Bti23od
Ento	2a3adto	Te2e3do	Bte2e3do
Hinne	2a3ado	Ye2e3do	Bye2e3do
Ne7na	2a3adna	Ni23od	Mni23od

	Imperative
2inta	23od
2inte	23ede
2into	23edo

	Active Participle
Masculine	2e3id
Feminine	2e3de
Plural	2e3din

2inte ktir bte2e3de, lezim ta3emle sport aktar
You sit alot, you should do more sports

Ento lezim te2e3do lamma tfooto 3al saf
You have to sit down when you enter the class

Hinne 2a3ado ma7al ma lezim ye2e3do
They sat down where they shouldn't have

23edo kelkon sawa
Sit down all of you

Hayye 2e3id 3ala l sofa
He is sitting on the sofa

To pay

	Perfect	Imperfect	Bi-imperfect
Ana	Dafa3it	2idfa3	Bidfa3
2inta	Dafa3it	Tidfa3	Btidfa3
2inte	Dafa3te	Tidfa3e	Btidfa3e
Howwe	Dafa3	Yidfa3	Byidfa3
Hiyye	Dafa3it	Tidfa3	Btidfa3
Ento	Dafa3to	Tidfa3o	Btidfa3o
Hinne	Dafa3o	Yidfa3o	Byidfa3o
Ne7na	Dafa3na	Nidfa3	Mnidfa3

	Imperative
2inta	Dfa3
2inte	Dfa3e
2into	Dfa3o

	Active Participle
Masculine	Defi3
Feminine	Def3a
Plural	Def3in

2inta dafa3it haydik l marra, hal marra ana bidfa3
You paid last time, this time I pay

Mafrood 3laykon tidfa3o lal maw2af kel shaher
You have to pay for the parking every month

Bas serna def3in ktir lyum!
We have paid a lot today!

Dfa3e 3anne lyom w ba3den birja3 ba3tike
Pay for me today and I will give you the money back later

Ana defi3 ba3ed fi howwe ma dafa3
I have paid, there's still him who hasn't paid yet

To hold

	Perfect	Imperfect	Bi-imperfect
Ana	Masakit	2imsok	Bimsok
2inta	Masakit	Timsok	Btimsok
2inte	Masakte	Temeske	Btemeske
Howwe	Masak	Yimsok	Byimsok
Hiyye	Masakit	Timsok	Btimsok
Ento	Masakto	Temesko	Btemesko
Hinne	Masako	Yemesko	Byemesko
Ne7na	Masakna	Nimsok	Mnimsok

	Imperative
2inta	Msok
2inte	Mseke
2into	Mseko

	Active Participle
Masculine	Mesik
Feminine	Meske
Plural	Meskin

Masakte l 7arame b e5ir la7za!
You caught the thief in the last second!

Hiyye lezim timsok 7ala shway
She should hold herself back a little

Mnimsok 2iden ba3ed lamma nitla3 3al saf
We hold each other's hands when we go to class

Ba3rid baddak tfoot 3al 7ammem bas mseka shway
I know you have to go to the toilet but hold it in a bit

Hiyye meske l saf kello
She holds the whole class

To ask

	Perfect	Imperfect	Bi-imperfect
Ana	Sa2alit	2is2al	Bis2al
2inta	Sa2alit	Tis2al	Btis2al
2inte	Sa2alte	Tis2ale	Btis2ale
Howwe	Sa2al	Yis2al	Byis2al
Hiyye	Sa2alit	Tis2al	Btis2al
Ento	Sa2alto	Tis2alo	Btis2alo
Hinne	Sa2alo	Yis2alo	Byis2alo
Ne7na	Sa2alna	Nis2al	Mnis2al

	Imperative
2inta	S2al
2inte	S2ale
2into	S2alo

	Active Participle
Masculine	Se2il
Feminine	Se2le
Plural	Se2lin

Ana 3atool bis2al l m3alme eza fi shi ma fhemto
I always ask the teacher if there's something I didn't understand

Howwe lezim yis2al adde l 7seb
He has to ask how much is the check

Sa2alna min wen mni2dar nishtre li3be bas ma 7ada se3adna
We asked where we could buy a game but no one helped us

S2alne w 5allisne
Ask me and let's get it over with

Toli3 se2il bel madrase eza bokra fi saf bas ma 2ije jaweb
He has asked the school if there's class tomorrow but didn't get an answer

To find

	Perfect	Imperfect	Bi-imperfect
Ana	La2et	Le2e	Ble2e
2inta	La2et	Tle2e	Bitle2e
2inte	La2ayte	Tle2e	Bitle2e
Howwe	Le2a	Yle2e	Bile2e
Hiyye	Le2it	Tle2e	Bitle2e
Ento	La2ayto	Tle2o	Bitle2o
Hinne	La2o	Yle2o	Bile2o
Ne7na	La2ayna	Nle2e	Minle2e

	Imperative
2inta	Le2e
2inte	Le2e
2into	Le2o

	Active Participle
Masculine	Mle2e
Feminine	Mle2ye
Plural	Mle2yin

Ana ble2e l film ktir 7elo
I find the movie very good

Howwe wa a5iran le2a l 2alam ken ta7et l tawle
He at last found the pen it was under the table

Hinne lezim yle2o 7al bser3a!
They must find a solution fast!

Le2ile l daftar bser3a
Find me the notebook fast

Ana mle2e eno hayda l 7al l monesib
I find that this is the best solution

To leave

	Perfect	Imperfect	Bi-imperfect
Ana	Tarakit	2itrok	Bitrok
2inta	Tarakit	Titrok	Btitrok
2inte	Tarakte	Teterke	Bteterke
Howwe	Tarak	Yitrok	Byitrok
Hiyye	Tarakit	Titrok	Btitrok
Ento	Tarakto	Teterko	Bteterko
Hinne	Tarako	Yeterko	Byeterko
Ne7na	Tarakna	Nitrok	Mnitrok

	Imperative
2inta	Trok
2inte	Treke
2into	Treko

	Active Participle
Masculine	Terik
Feminine	Terke
Plural	Terkin

Tarakna ana weyyeha
We left each other

Le tarakto l sa7en 3al tawle?
Why did you leave the plate on the table?

2alle 2itrok ra2me w enno 7a yde2elle
He told me to leave my number and that he will call me

Treko kel shi 3am ta3emlo w ta3o la hon!
Leave everything you are doing and come here!

Sarlon shi shahren terkin ba3ed
They have left each other about two months ago

To hear

	Perfect	Imperfect	Bi-imperfect
Ana	Sme3et	2isma3	Bisma3
2inta	Sme3et	Tisma3	Btisma3
2inte	Smi3te	Tisma3e	Btisma3e
Howwe	Seme3	Yisma3	Byisma3
Hiyye	Sim3it	Tisma3	Btisma3
Ento	Sme3to	Tisma3o	Btisma3o
Hinne	Sem3o	Yisma3o	Byisma3o
Ne7na	Sme3na	Nisma3	Mnisma3

Imperative	
2inta	Sma3
2inte	Sma3e
2into	Sma3o

Active Participle	
Masculine	Semi3
Feminine	Sem3a
Plural	Sem3in

Ana bisma3 mosee2a kel yom l sobo7
I hear music everyday morning

Lezim tisma3e abel ma tjewbe
You have to fear before you answer

Hinne sem3o eno bokra 3otle
They heard that tomorrow is a holiday

Sma3 hal ghiniyye lal 2e5ir
Hear this song to the end

Ma ba2a teje 3ala hal 7ay, semi3?!
Don't come to this neighborhood again, you hear?!

To lie

	Perfect	Imperfect	Bi-imperfect
Ana	Kazzabit	Kazzib	Bkazzib
2inta	Kazzabit	Tkazzib	Bitkazzib
2inte	Kazzabte	Tkazbe	Bitkazbe
Howwe	Kazzab	Ykazzib	Bikazzib
Hiyye	Kazzabit	Tkazzib	Bitkazzib
Ento	Kazzabto	Tkazbo	Bitkazbo
Hinne	Kazzabo	Ykazbo	Bikazbo
Ne7na	Kazzabna	Nkazzib	Minkazzib

	Imperative
2inta	Kazzib
2inte	Kazbe
2into	Kazbo

	Active Participle
Masculine	Mkazzib
Feminine	Mkazbe
Plural	Mkazbin

Eza bitkazzib 3layye lezim ta3tine masare
If you like then you'll have to give money

Ma lezim tkazzib 3ala ahla
She must not lie to her parents

Ne7na wala marra kazzabna 3ala l siyesiyye bas hinne 3atool bikazbo 3layna
We never lied to the politicians but they always lie to us

Kazbe 3le w 2elilo eno meshe l7al
Lie to him and say that it worked

Toli3 mkazzib 3layye w ana ma 3arfen!
He has lied to me and I didn't know that!

To arrive

	Perfect	Imperfect	Bi-imperfect
Ana	Wsolet	2ousal	Bousal
2inta	Wsolet	Tousal	Btousal
2inte	Wsolte	Tousale	Btousale
Howwe	Wosil	Yousal	Byousal
Hiyye	Woslit	Tousal	Btousal
Ento	Wsolto	Tousalo	Btousalo
Hinne	Woslo	Yousalo	Byousalo
Ne7na	Wsolna	Nousal	Mnousal

	Imperative
2inta	Wsaal
2inte	Wsale
2into	Wsalo

	Active Participle
Masculine	Waasil
Feminine	Waasle
Plural	Waaslin

Ana shakle ra7 2ousal bakkir
It appears that I will arrive early

3adatan byousal kel yom 3al se3a 3ashra
He usually arrives every day at ten

Woslo aw ba3ed?
Did they arrive or not yet

Wsaal 3ala mafra2 Khalde w di2ille
Arrive at Khalde's turn and then call me

Hayyene seret waasil
I am about to arrive

To call

	Perfect	Imperfect	Bi-imperfect
Ana	Talfanit	Talfin	Btalfin
2inta	Talfanit	Ttalfin	Bittalfin
2inte	Talfante	Ttalifne	bittalifne
Howwe	Talfan	Ytalfin	Bitalfin
Hiyye	Talfanit	Ttalfin	Bittalfin
Ento	Talfanto	Ttalefno	Bittalefno
Hinne	Talfano	Ytalefno	Bitalefno
Ne7na	Talfanna	Ntalfin	Mintalfin

	Imperative
2inta	Talfin
2inte	Talifne
2into	Talefno

	Active Participle
Masculine	Mtalfin
Feminine	Mtalifne
Plural	Mtalfnin

Talfantilo walla ba3ed?
Did you call him or not yet?

Hiyye lezim ttalfin la te5od maw3ad
She has to call to make an appointment

3am mintalfin sarelna min mberi7 w ma 7ada 3am b rid
We have been calling since yesterday and no one is picking up

Talefnoolo w 2oloolo eno ne7na jeyin
Call him and tell him we are coming

Toli3 mtalfinlo w ma 2ayille
He has called him but didn't tell me

To earn

	Perfect	Imperfect	Bi-imperfect
Ana	2abadit	2i2bad	Bi2bad
2inta	2abadit	Ti2bad	Bti2bad
2inte	2abadte	Ti2bade	Bti2bade
Howwe	2abad	Yi2bad	Byi2bad
Hiyye	2abadit	Ti2bad	Bti2bad
Ento	2abadto	Ti2bado	Bti2bado
Hinne	2abado	Yi2bado	Byi2bado
Ne7na	2abadna	Ni2bad	Mni2bad

	Imperative
2inta	2baad
2inte	2bade
2into	2bado

	Active Participle
Masculine	2aabid
Feminine	2aabda
Plural	2aabdin

Ana bi2bad kel 2e5ir shaher
I get paid every last of the month

Hiyye 2abadit 3ala sheghla
She got paid on her work

Ne7na sar lezim ni2bad lyum
We must get paid today

2bade dighre w ma tontre
Get paid quick and don't wait

Hinne 2aabdin 3ala sheghlon min abel
They have been paid on their work before

To promise

	Perfect	Imperfect	Bi-imperfect
Ana	Wa3adit	2ou3id	Bou3id
2inta	Wa3adit	Tou3id	Btou3id
2inte	Wa3adte	Tou3de	Btou3de
Howwe	Wa3ad	You3id	Byou3id
Hiyye	Wa3adit	Tou3id	Btou3id
Ento	Wa3adto	Tou3do	Btou3do
Hinne	Wa3ado	You3ado	Byou3ado
Ne7na	Wa3adna	Nou3id	Mnou3id

Imperative	
2inta	W3od
2inte	W3ade
2into	W3odo

Active Participle	
Masculine	We3id
Feminine	We3de
Plural	We3din

Ana bou3dak enno ra7 eje bokra l sobo7
I promise you I will come tomorrow morning

Ente wa3adtine eno tde2ile abel ma tneme
You promised to call me before you go to sleep

Hinne lezim you3do mwazzafinon ya3towon masare 3a 3id l miled
They have to promise their employees to give them money on Christmas

W3idne eno ma tinsene
Promise me you'll not forget me

Hinne we3dinna eno yejo lyum
They have promised us that they are coming today

To walk

	Perfect	Imperfect	Bi-imperfect
Ana	Mshit	2imshe	Bimshe
2inta	Mshit	Timshe	Btimshe
2inte	Mshite	Timshe	Btimshe
Howwe	Meshe	Yimshe	Byimshe
Hiyye	Mishyit	Timshe	Btimshe
Ento	Mishyo	Timsho	Btimsho
Hinne	Mesho	Yimsho	Byimsho
Ne7na	Mshina	Nimshe	Mnimshe

Imperative	
2inta	2imshe
2inte	2imshe
2into	2imsho

Active Participle	
Masculine	Meshe
Feminine	Meshye
Plural	Meshyin

Bas tousal 3al bet 2ille la 2imshe la 3andak
When you get home tell me to walk to your place

Hiyye btimshe kel yom shi 3ashra kilometer
She walks every day about 10 kilometers

L sheri3 ken msakkar 2imna mshina la nousal lal sheghel
The road was blocked so we walked to reach the work

2om 2imshe la thaddim
Go walk to digest

Battal feya tit7ammal sarit meshye ktir lyum
She can't take it anymore she has walked a lot today

To celebrate

	Perfect	Imperfect	Bi-imperfect
Ana	7tafalit	2i7tifil	Bti7tifil
2inta	7tafalit	Ti7tifil	Bti7tifil
2inte	7tafalte	Ti7tifle	Bti7tifle
Howwe	7tafal	Yi7tifil	Byi7tifil
Hiyye	7tafalit	Ti7tifil	Bti7tifil
Ento	7tafalto	Ti7teflo	Bti7teflo
Hinne	7tafalo	Yi7teflo	Byi7teflo
Ne7na	7tafalna	Ni7tefel	Mni7tefel

	Imperative
2inta	7tefel
2inte	7tifle
2into	7tiflo

	Active Participle
Masculine	Mi7tifil
Feminine	Mi7tifle
Plural	Mi7tiflin

Ana m2akkad ra7 2inja7 bel 2emti7an fa lezim 2i7tifil
I am sure I will succeed in the exam so I have to celebrate

Howwe 7tafal lamma marto 5allafit
He celebrated when his wife gave birth

Bti7teflo b 3id l miled?
Do you celebrate Christmas?

Ana jeet yalla 7tiflo
I am here come on celebrate

Trou7 la 3and Randa? Mi7tifle b 3eeda lyum
Shall we go to Randa's place? She's celebrating her birthday today

To invite

	Perfect	Imperfect	Bi-imperfect
Ana	3azamit	2i3zom	Bi3zom
2inta	3azamit	Ti3zom	Bti3zom
2inte	3azamte	Te3ezme	Bte3ezme
Howwe	3azam	Yi3zom	Byi3zom
Hiyye	3azamit	Ti3zom	Bti3zom
Ento	3azamto	Te3ezmo	Bte3ezmo
Hinne	3azamo	Ye3ezmo	Bye3ezmo
Ne7na	3azamna	Ni3zom	Mne3zom

	Imperative
2inta	3zom
2inte	3zeme
2into	3zemo

	Active Participle
Masculine	3aazim
Feminine	3aazme
Plural	3aazmin

Ana bi3zom ktir 3alam w 2e5ir hamme l masare
I invite alot of people and I don't care about money

Howwe lezim yi3zom rfi2o 3ala l 3asha
He should invite his friend to dinner

Hiyye 3azametna 3ala 7seba
She invited us on her treat

3zom ya3ne adde sarlak ma 3azimne
Invite me, how long has it been since you've invited me

Sarit 3aazme nos l saf
She has invited half of the class

To show

	Perfect	Imperfect	Bi-imperfect
Ana	Farjet	Farje	Bfarje
2inta	Farjet	Tfarje	Bitfarje
2inte	Farjayte	Tfarje	Bitfarje
Howwe	Farja	Yfarje	Bifarje
Hiyye	Farjit	Tfarje	Bitfarje
Ento	Farjayto	Tfarjo	Bitfarjo
Hinne	Farjo	Yfarjo	Bifarjo
Ne7na	Farjayna	Nfarje	Minfarje

	Imperative
2inta	Farje
2inte	Farje
2into	Farjo

	Active Participle
Masculine	Mfarje
Feminine	Mfarjiyye
Plural	Mfarjiyyin

Farjine eza 3andak daleel
Show me if you have evidence

Hiyye farjit ahla enno nej7a bel 2emti7an
She showed her parents that she passed the exam

Lezim yfarjo eno mamnoo3 yi7ko hek
They should show him that he shouldn't talk like that

Ana bfarje 2adde seret 3amel bel 7ayet
I show how much I have done in life

Howwe mfarjo 7alo eno howe l mni7
He shows himself as if he's the good guy

To feel

	Perfect	Imperfect	Bi-imperfect
Ana	7asset	7is	B7is
2inta	7asset	T7is	Bit7is
2inte	7assayte	T7isse	Bit7isse
Howwe	7as	Y7is	Bi7is
Hiyye	7assit	T7is	Bit7is
Ento	7assayto	T7isso	Bit7isso
Hinne	7asso	Y7isso	Bi7esso
Ne7na	7assayna	N7is	Min7is

	Imperative
2inta	7is
2inte	7isse
2into	7isso

	Active Participle
Masculine	7asis
Feminine	7asse
Plural	7assin

7asis eno 7a ysir shi ma mni7 b hal yawmen
I feel that something bad will happen these two days

7is fiyye shway!
Feel with me a bit!

7assayte 7alik shi ma5noo2a min ba3ed hal 7adse?
Do you feel chocked after this incident?

Lezim y7isso eno 3emlo shi ghalat
They have to feel that they did something wrong

Bit7is 7alak eno fik laya hal shaghle?
Do you feel that you are up to it?

To close

	Perfect	Imperfect	Bi-imperfect
Ana	Sakkarit	Sakkir	Bsakkir
2inta	Sakkarit	Tsakkir	Bitsakkir
2inte	Sakkarte	Tsakre	Bitsakre
Howwe	Sakkar	Ysakkir	Bisakkir
Hiyye	Sakkarit	Tsakkir	Bitsakkir
Ento	Sakkarto	Tsakro	Bitsakro
Hinne	Sakkaro	Ysakro	Bisakro
Ne7na	Sakkarna	Nsakkir	Minsakkir

Imperative	
2inta	Sakkir
2inte	Sakre
2into	Sakro

Active Participle	
Masculine	Msakkar
Feminine	Msakre
Plural	Msakrin

Ana bsakkir l ma7al kel yom 3al se3a 5amse
I close the shop every day at five

Ma tsakre l beb halla2 la7za hayyene jeye
Don't close the door now, wait I'm coming

Hinne sakkaro l sheri3 3layna
They closed the streets on us

Sakkir l shibbek, ktir bared!
Close the window, it's very cold!

La halla2 msakrin, bokra byifta7o
No they have closed for now, they open tomorrow

To bring

	Perfect	Imperfect	Bi-imperfect
Ana	Jebet	Jib	Bjib
2inta	Jebet	Tjib	Bitjib
2inte	Jibte	Tjibe	Bitjibe
Howwe	Jeb	Yjib	Bijib
Hiyye	Jebit	Tjib	Bitjib
Ento	Jebto	Tjibo	Bitjibo
Hinne	Jebo	Yjibo	Bijibo
Ne7na	Jebna	Njib	Minjib

	Imperative
2inta	Jib
2inte	Jibe
2into	Jibo

	Active Participle
Masculine	Jeyib
Feminine	Jeybe
Plural	Jeybin

Howwe bijib kel yom 3elebten do5an
He brings every day two packs of cigarettes

Lezim tjibo ma3kon Khaled
You have to bring Khaled with you

Jina w jebna l 3arous w jina
We came and brought the bride with us

Jib ma3ak kees batata
Bring potato chips with you

Tol3it jeybe ma3a akla ma3a
She has brought her own food with her

To change

	Perfect	Imperfect	Bi-imperfect
Ana	Ghayyarit	Ghayyir	Bghayyir
2inta	Ghayyarit	Tghayyir	Bitghayyir
2inte	Ghayyarte	Tghayre	Bitghayre
Howwe	Ghayyar	Ghayyir	Bighayyir
Hiyye	Ghayyarit	Tghayyir	Bitghayyir
Ento	Ghayyarto	Tghayro	Bitghayro
Hinne	Ghayyaro	Yghayro	Bighayro
Ne7na	Ghayyarna	Nghayyir	Minghayyir

Imperative	
2inta	Ghayyir
2inte	Ghayre
2into	Ghayro

Active Participle	
Masculine	Mghayyir
Feminine	Mghayra
Plural	Mghayrin

Ana bghayyir filter l aquarium kel shaher
I change the aquarium filter every month

Hiyye ghayyarit 2i5tisasa
She changed her major

Lezim nghayyir l nizam
We have to change the system

Ghayyir l kanze tal3a ri7eta!
Change the shirt it stinks!

Tol3o mghayrin l fetoura w ana ma 3arfen
They have changed the receipt and I didn't know about it

To see

	Perfect	Imperfect	Bi-imperfect
Ana	Shefet	Shoof	Bshoof
2inta	Shefet	Tshoof	Bitshoof
2inte	Shifte	Tshoofe	Bitshoofe
Howwe	Shef	Yshoof	Bishoof
Hiyye	Shefit	Tshoof	Bitshoof
Ento	Shefto	Tshoofo	Bitshoofo
Hinne	Shefo	Yshoofo	Bishoofo
Ne7na	Shefna	Nshoof	Minshoof

	Imperative
2inta	Shoof
2inte	Shoofe
2into	Shoofo

	Active Participle
Masculine	Sheyif
Feminine	Sheyfe
Plural	Sheyfin

Ana bshoof eno kel shi meshe tamem
I am seeing that everything is working just fine

Howwe lezim yshoof eza ma3o wa2et
He has to see if he has time

Hiyye shefit eno ma ba2a 7a tla77i2
She saw that she can't make it on time

Shoof sho fi hon
Look what is here

Hiyye sheyfe eno byimshe l7al
She sees that it will work out

To drink

	Perfect	Imperfect	Bi-imperfect
Ana	Shrebet	2ishrab	Bishrab
2inta	Shrebet	Tishrab	Btishrab
2inte	Shribte	Tishrabe	Btishrabe
Howwe	Shereb	Yishrab	Byishrab
Hiyye	Shirbit	Tishrab	Btishrab
Ento	Shrebto	Tishrabo	Bteshrabo
Hinne	Sherbo	Yishrabo	Byishrabo
Ne7na	Shrebna	Nishrab	Mnishrab

	Imperative
2inta	Shraab
2inte	Shrabe
2into	Shrabo

	Active Participle
Masculine	Sherib
Feminine	Sherbe
Plural	Sherbin

Ana ma bishrab ko7ool
I don't drink alcohol

Hiyye lezim tishrab kel yom anninten may
She has to drink everyday two bottles of water

Sherbo shi 2anninten beera
They drank like two beers

Shraab ahwe ma3e
Drink coffee with me

Ma ba2a ta3ti annine tenye, sar sherib ktir!
Don't give him another bottle, he has drank a lot!

To work

	Perfect	Imperfect	Bi-imperfect
Ana	Shtaghalet	2ishteghel	Bishteghel
2inta	Shtaghalet	Tishteghel	Btishteghel
2inte	Shtaghalte	Tishteghle	Btishteghle
Howwe	Shtaghal	Yishteghel	Byishteghel
Hiyye	Shtaghalit	Tishteghel	Btishteghel
Ento	Shtaghalto	Tishteghlo	Btishteghlo
Hinne	Shtaghalo	Yishteghlo	Byishteghlo
Ne7na	Shtaghalna	Nishteghel	Mnishteghel

	Imperative
2inta	Shteghel
2inte	Shtighle
2into	Shtighlo

	Active Participle
Masculine	Mishteghel
Feminine	Mishtighle
Plural	Mishtighlin

Hiyye btishteghel kel yom shi tman se3at
She works every day for eight hours

Ana lezim 2ishteghel 3ala ktebe l jdid
I have to work on my new book

Ne7na shtaghalna kelna sawa 3ala hal mashrou3
We all have worked together on this project

Shteghel la tousal la natije
Work till you get to a result

Hiyye mishtighle 3ala 7ala ktir
She has worked on herself a lot

To treat

	Perfect	Imperfect	Bi-imperfect
Ana	T3amalit	2it3amal	Bit3amal
2inta	T3amalit	Tit3amal	Btit3amal
2inte	T3amalte	Tit3amale	Btit3amale
Howwe	T3amal	Yit3amal	Byit3amal
Hiyye	T3amalit	Tit3amal	Btit3amal
Ento	T3amalto	Tit3amalo	Btit3amalo
Hinne	T3amalo	Yit3amalo	Byit3amalo
Ne7na	T3amalna	Nit3amal	Mnit3amal

Imperative	
2inta	T3amal
2inte	T3amale
2into	T3amalo

Active Participle	
Masculine	Mit3amal
Feminine	Mit3amle
Plural	Mit3amlin

Lezim tit3amal ma3 l 3alam b tari2a mni7a
You have to treat people in a good way

Hiyye t3amalit ma3e b tari2a bish3a
She treated ma3e in a very bad way

Ahamma shi eno nit3amal ma3on b tari2a 2i7tirafiyye
The most important thing is for us to treat them in a professional way

T3amal ma3e ka2ane sa7bak
Treat me as if I'm your best friend

2aloole eno mit3amal ma3a b tari2a bish3a
I have been told that he has treated her in an ugly way

To put

	Perfect	Imperfect	Bi-imperfect
Ana	7attet	7ot	B7ot
2inta	7attet	T7ot	Bit7ot
2inte	7attayte	T7otte	Bit7otte
Howwe	7at	Y7ot	Bi7ot
Hiyye	7attit	T7ot	Bit7ot
Ento	7attayto	T7otto	Bit7otto
Hinne	7atto	Y7otto	Bi7otto
Ne7na	7attayna	N7ot	Min7ot

Imperative	
2inta	7ot
2inte	7otte
2into	7otto

Active Participle	
Masculine	7atit
Feminine	7atta
Plural	7attin

Enta bit7ot 7alak b mawa2if bey5a
You put yourself in stupid situations

Howwe lezim y7ot ra2mo bel CV
He has to put his number in his resume

Hiyye 7attit 7ala 2iddem l ra2ey l 3am
She put herself in front of the public opinion

7ot 2idek w 2ijrek b may berde
Put your hands and feet in cold water

Hiyye 7atta 3alam libnen 3ala l baranda
She has put the Lebanese flag on the balcony

To use

	Perfect	Imperfect	Bi-imperfect
Ana	Sta3malit	Sta3mil	Bista3mil
2inta	Sta3malit	Tista3mil	Btista3mil
2inte	Sta3malte	Tista3emle	Btista3emle
Howwe	Sta3mal	Yista3mil	Byista3mil
Hiyye	Sta3malit	Tista3mil	Btista3mil
Ento	Sta3malto	Tista3emlo	Btista3emlo
Hinne	Sta3malo	Yista3emlo	Byista3emlo
Ne7na	Sta3malna	Nista3mil	Mnista3mil

	Imperative
2inta	Sta3mil
2inte	Sta3imle
2into	Sta3emlo

	Active Participle
Masculine	Mista3mil
Feminine	Mista3imle
Plural	Mista3imlin

Mokefa7it l shaghab 3am yista3emlo kanebil mosayile lil dmoo3
Riot police are using tear gases

Hiyye sta3malit kilme ma ken lezim tista3mela
She used a word she wasn't supposed to use

Ne7na ma mnista3mil l sle7
We don't use weapons

Sta3imle 2owtik bel sheghel
Use your power in work

Tol3o mitsa3emlin mo5addarat bel night
It appears they have used drugs in the club

To request

	Perfect	Imperfect	Bi-imperfect
Ana	Talabit	2itlob	Bitlob
2inta	Talabit	Titlob	Btitlob
2inte	Talabte	Totolbe	Btotolbe
Howwe	Talab	Yotlob	Byotlob
Hiyye	Talabit	Titlob	Btitlob
Ento	Talabto	Totolbo	Btotolbo
Hinne	Talabo	Yotolbo	Byotolbo
Ne7na	Talabna	Nitlob	Mnotlob

Imperative	
2inta	Tlob
2inte	Tlobe
2into	Tlobo

Active Participle	
Masculine	Taalib
Feminine	Taalbe
Plural	Taalbin

Ana bitlob min l kil l tlemiz eno ma yroo7o 3al saf
I request all the students to not go to class

Howwe lezim yotlob 2izna abel ma yitsarraf
He must request her permission before taking action

Shi marra talabto minne shi w 2elet la2?
Have you ever requested something from me and said no?

Tlob w tmanna
Request and wish

Hiyye taalbe eno tit7a22a2 kil mataaleba
She has requested that all her demands shall be fulfilled

To laugh

	Perfect	Imperfect	Bi-imperfect
Ana	D7okit	2id7ak	Bid7ak
2inta	D7okit	Tid7ak	Btid7ak
2inte	D7okte	Tid7ake	Btid7ake
Howwe	Do7ik	Yid7ak	Byid7ak
Hiyye	Do7kit	Tid7ak	Btid7ak
Ento	D7okto	Tid7ako	Btid7ako
Hinne	Do7ko	Yid7ako	Byid7ako
Ne7na	D7okna	Nid7ak	Mnid7ak

Imperative	
2inta	D7ak
2inte	D7ake
2into	D7ako

Active Participle	
Masculine	Daa7ik
Feminine	Daa7ke
Plural	Daa7kin

Ana bid7ak 3ala siyesit libnen
I laugh at the Lebanese politics

Hiyye do7kit 3ala l nikte
She laughed at the joke

Hinne akid 7a yid7ako lamma yisma3o l 5abar
They will for sure laugh when they hear the news

D7ako shway 7aje 3ebsin
Laugh a little stop frowning

Tol3o daa7kin 3layna kelna
They appeared they have laughed at all of us

To understand

	Perfect	Imperfect	Bi-imperfect
Ana	Fhemet	2ifham	Bifham
2inta	Fhemet	Tifham	Btifham
2inte	Fhimte	Tifhame	Btifhame
Howwe	Fehem	Yifham	Byifham
Hiyye	Fihmit	Tifham	Btifham
Ento	Fhemto	Tifhamo	Btifhamo
Hinne	Fehmo	Yifhamo	Byifhamo
Ne7na	Fhimna	Nifham	Mnifham

	Imperative
2inta	Fham
2inte	Fhame
2into	Fhamo

	Active Participle
Masculine	Fehim
Feminine	Fehme
Plural	Fehmin

Fhemet sho azde lamma eltellak hek?
Did you understand what I mean when I told you this?

Hiyye ma ra7 tifham 2ella ma de2ella w i7keya
She will not understand until I call her and talk to her

Hinne byifhamowa 3al tayer
They understand it very quick

Fhame l mawdou3 abel ma te7kine
Understand the subject before you talk to me

Ente shaklik fehme l mawdoo3 ghalat
It seems you have misunderstood the subject

To fall

	Perfect	Imperfect	Bi-imperfect
Ana	W2e3et	2ou2a3	Bou2a3
2inta	W2e3et	Tou2a3	Btou2a3
2inte	W2i3te	Tou2a3e	Btou2a3e
Howwe	We2e3	You2a3	Byou2a3
Hiyye	Wi23it	Tou2a3	Btou2a3
Ento	W2e3to	Tou2a3o	Btou2a3o
Hinne	We23o	You2a3o	Byou2a3o
Ne7na	W2e3na	Nou2a3	Mnou2a3

	Imperative
2inta	W2aa3
2inte	W2a3e
2into	W2a3o

	Active Participle
Masculine	We2i3
Feminine	We23a
Plural	We23in

We23a bel 7ob fi 3al 2e5ir
She has fallen very deeply in love with him

W2aa3 la tirja3 ta3rif tish2ol 7alak
Fall down to know how to lift yourself up again

Kellon we23o bel fa5
They all fell in the trap

Ntebeh l msajle ra7 tou2a3!
Watch out the radio is gonna fall!

Ana kel marra bitfarkash b hal 7affe w bou2a3
Everytime I trip on this edge and fall down

To avoid

	Perfect	Imperfect	Bi-imperfect
Ana	Tfedet	2itfeda	Bitfeda
2inta	Tfedet	Titfeda	Bitfeda
2inte	Tfedayte	Titfede	Btitfede
Howwe	Tfeda	Yitfeda	Byitfeda
Hiyye	Tfedit	Titfeda	Btitfeda
Ento	Tfedayto	Titfedo	Btitfedo
Hinne	Tfedo	Yitfedo	Byitfedo
Ne7na	Tfedayna	Nitfeda	Mnitfeda

Imperative	
2inta	Tfeda
2inte	Tfede
2into	Tfedo

Active Participle	
Masculine	Mitfede
Feminine	Mitfedye
Plural	Mitfedyin

Kelna lezim nitfeda hal mashkal!
We must all avoid this fight!

Hiyye tfedit l 7adis 3ala 2e5ir la7za
She avoided the accident in the last moment

Hiyye btitfeda timro2 min haydak l 7ay bel lel
She avoids passing by that neighborhood at night

Tfeda tit3ata ma3e la fatra
Avoid talking to me for a while

Howwe mitfede yimro2 min 2iddem l ma5far
He has avoided passing by the police station

To thank

	Perfect	Imperfect	Bi-imperfect
Ana	Shakarit	2ishkor	Bishkor
2inta	Shakarit	Tishkor	Btishkor
2inte	Shakarte	Teshekre	Bteshekre
Howwe	Shakar	Yishkor	Byishkor
Hiyye	Shakarit	Tishkor	Btishkor
Ento	Shakarto	Teshkro	Bteshkro
Hinne	Shakaro	Yishkro	Byishkro
Ne7na	Shakarna	Nishkor	Mnishkor

Imperative	
2inta	Shkor
2inte	Shkere
2into	Shkero

Active Participle	
Masculine	Shekir
Feminine	Shekra
Plural	Shekrin

Ana b7ib 2ishkor kil rif2ate lle 2ejo 3ala l 7afle
I would like to thank all my friends that came to the party

2inte ktir bteshekre l 3alam
You thank the people a lot

Ne7na shakarna kil le se3adna b terkib l masra7
We thanked all that helped us in putting up the stage

Shkere rabbik mir2it 3a 5er!
Thank your God that it went well!

Kelna shekrin Allah 3a kil shi
We all thank God for everything

Have lunch

	Perfect	Imperfect	Bi-imperfect
Ana	Tghaddet	2itghadda	Bitghadda
2inta	Tghaddet	Titghadda	Btitghadda
2inte	Tghaddayte	Titghadde	Btitghadde
Howwe	Tghadda	Yitghadda	Byitghadda
Hiyye	Tghaddit	Titghadda	Btitghadda
Ento	Tghaddo	Titghaddo	Btitghaddo
Hinne	Tghaddo	Yitghaddo	Byitghaddo
Ne7na	Tghaddayna	Nitghadda	Mnitghadda

	Imperative
2inta	Tghadda
2inte	Tghadde
2into	Tghaddo

	Active Participle
Masculine	Mitghadde
Feminine	Mitghadye
Plural	Mitghadyin

Ana bitghadda kel yom 3al se3a tlete
I have lunch every day at three

Ma byiswa titghadda kel yom barra
It's not healthy to have lunch outside every day

Ma daroore na3mil akel, tghaddo abel ma yejo la 3anna
We don't need to cook, they had lunch before they came here

Tghadde w ta3e la 3ande
Have lunch and then come to my place

La merci ana mitghadde bel bet
No thank you I had lunch at home

To touch

	Perfect	Imperfect	Bi-imperfect
Ana	Da2arit	2id2ar	Bid2ar
2inta	Da2arit	Tid2ar	Btid2ar
2inte	Da2arte	Tid2are	Btid2are
Howwe	Da2ar	Yid2ar	Byid2ar
Hiyye	Da2arit	Tid2ar	Byid2ar
Ento	Da2arto	Tid2aro	Btid2aro
Hinne	Da2aro	Yid2aro	Byid2aro
Ne7na	Da2arna	Nid2ar	Mnid2ar

	Imperative
2inta	D2ar
2inte	D2are
2into	D2aro

	Active Participle
Masculine	De2ir
Feminine	De2ra
Plural	De2rin

Ana ma bid2ar shi mish masmi7le 2id2aro
I don't touch something I am not allowed to touch

Foote ghasle 2idayke, da2arte manshafe wes5a
Go wash your hands, you touched a dirty towel

Lezim nintebeh sho nid2ar, fi ktir 2ishya b2alba microbet
We have to watch out what we touch, there are a lot of stuff that has bacteria

D2ar fiye w shoof sho bisir fik
Touch me and see what will happen with you

Toli3 mzammir jihez l 2inzar la2ano de2ra law7a mamnoo3 tid2ara
The alarm has sounded because she has touched a painting which she's not allowed to touch

To take

	Perfect	Imperfect	Bi-imperfect
Ana	2a5adet	2e5od	Be5od
2inta	2a5adet	Te5od	Bte5od
2inte	2a5adte	Te5de	Bte5de
Howwe	2a5ad	Ye5od	Bye5od
Hiyye	2a5adit	Te5od	Bte5od
Ento	2a5adto	Te5do	Bte5do
Hinne	2a5ado	Ye5do	Bye5do
Ne7na	2a5adna	Ne5od	Mne5od

	Imperative
2inta	5od
2inte	5ede
2into	5edo

	Active Participle
Masculine	Me5id
Feminine	Me5de
Plural	Me5din

Ana be5od masroofe kel jom3a
I take my allowance every week

Lezim te5de 72oo2ik
You have to take your rights

Hinne bye5do taxi la yousalo 3a Beirut
They take a taxi to get to Beirut

5od hal masare w jible 3ilbit do55an
Take this money and get me a pack of cigarettes

Tol3it me5de bikslette e5ta
She has taken her sister's bicycle

To be

	Perfect	Imperfect	Bi-imperfect
Ana	Kenet	Koon	Bkoon
2inta	Kenet	Tkoone	Bitkoone
2inte	Kinte	Tkoone	Bitkoone
Howwe	Ken	Ykoon	Bikoon
Hiyye	Kenit	Tkoon	Bitkoon
Ento	Kento	Tkoono	Bitkoono
Hinne	Keno	Ykoono	Bikoono
Ne7na	Kenna	Nkoon	Minkoon

	Imperative
2inta	Koon
2inte	Koone
2into	Koono

	Active Participle
Masculine	Keyin
Feminine	Keyne
Plural	Keynin

Ana kenet we2if honik lamma sar hek
I was standing there when that happened

Ente shaklik 7a tkoone l mas2oole 3an l majmoo3a
It looks like you will be responsible of the group

Shi 5ames d2ayi2 w mnimshe, bitkoono ento wsolto
We will go in around five minutes, you have arrived there

Koon 3ande 3al se3a tinten
Be at my place at two

Hiyye keyne mghatteye 3le
She has had covered on him

To let

	Perfect	Imperfect	Bi-imperfect
Ana	5allet	5alle	B5alle
2inta	5allet	T5alle	Bit5alle
2inte	5allayte	T5alle	Bit5alle
Howwe	5alla	Y5alle	Bi5alle
Hiyye	5allit	T5alle	Bit5alle
Ento	5allayto	T5allo	Bit5allo
Hinne	5allo	Y5allo	Bi5allo
Ne7na	5allayna	N5alle	Min5alle

Imperative	
2inta	5alle
2inte	5alle
2into	5allo

Active Participle	
Masculine	M5alle
Feminine	M5alye
Plural	M5alyin

Ana lle b5alle hal 2arar yimro2 aw la2
I am the one who let this decision pass or not

Hiyye ra7 t5alle l seyara timro2
She will let the car pass

5allayna l 7okoome tista2eel ba3ed 2esboo3
We let the government resign after a week

5alleya til3ab shway
Let her play a little

M5alyin l daw mdawwa la yi2sha3o
They let the lights on to see

To join

	Perfect	Imperfect	Bi-imperfect
Ana	Ndammet	2indam	Bindam
2inta	Ndammet	Tindam	Btindam
2inte	Ndammayte	Tindamme	Btindamme
Howwe	Ndam	Yindam	Byindam
Hiyye	Ndammit	Tindam	Btindam
Ento	Ndammayto	Tindammo	Btindammo
Hinne	Ndammo	Yindammo	Byindammo
Ne7na	Ndammayna	Nindam	Mnindam

Imperative	
2inta	Ndam
2inte	Ndamme
2into	Ndammo

Active Participle	
Masculine	Mindam
Feminine	Mindamme
Plural	Mindammin

Ana manne mindam la wala 7ezeb
I have not joined any party

Ndamme lal jam3iyye la yitla3lik 7osoomet
Join our community to get coupons

Howwe nedem eno ndam la hal jam3iyye
He regretted that he joined this community

Ba3ed ma3kon 5ames d2ayi2 la tsajlo 2asameekon w tindammo
You still have five minutes to sign up and join

3teyon shawayet masare byindammo deghre
Give them a bit of money then they will join

To do

	Perfect	Imperfect	Bi-imperfect
Ana	3melet	2a3mil	Ba3mil
2inta	3melet	Ta3mil	Bta3mil
2inte	3milte	Ta3imle	Bta3imle
Howwe	3emel	Ya3mil	Bya3mil
Hiyye	3imlit	Ta3mil	Bta3mil
Ento	3melto	Ta3emlo	Bta3emlo
Hinne	3emlo	Ya3emlo	Bya3emlo
Ne7na	3melna	Na3mil	Mna3mil

	Imperative
2inta	3mol
2inte	3mele
2into	3melo

	Active Participle
Masculine	3aamil
Feminine	3aamle
Plural	3aamlin

Layke kif bta3emleya lal akle
Look how you do this dish

Ma lezim ta3emlo hek osas!
You should not do these kinds of stuff!

Law 3melna hek, ma ken 7ada wosil 3a bayto
If we did this, no one would have arrived home

3mele shi bi5allike tifti5re b7alik
Do something that makes you proud of yourself

Sho 3amlin?
What are you doing?

To ride

	Perfect	Imperfect	Bi-imperfect
Ana	Rkebet	2irkab	Birkab
2inta	Rkebet	Tirkab	Btirkab
2inte	Rkibte	Tirkabe	Btirkabe
Howwe	Rekeb	Yirkab	Byirkab
Hiyye	Rikbit	Tirkab	Btirkab
Ento	Rkebto	Tirkabo	Btirkabo
Hinne	Rekbo	Yirkabo	Byirkabo
Ne7na	Rkebna	Nirkab	Mnirkab

	Imperative
2inta	Rkab
2inte	Rkabe
2into	Rkabo

	Active Participle
Masculine	Rekib
Feminine	Rekbe
Plural	Rekbin

Ana birkab l bus kel yom
I ride the bus every day

Ta3o nirkab hayde l mawje
Let's ride this wave

Howe rikib l bisklette min hon la Saida
He rode the bike from here to Saida

Rkabo ma3e eza badkon
Ride with me if you want to

Tol3o rekbin abel bel tren l majnoon
They had already ridden the roller coaster before

To announce

	Perfect	Imperfect	Bi-imperfect
Ana	2a3lanit	2o3lon	Bo3lon
2inta	2a3lanit	To3lon	Bto3lon
2inte	2a3lante	Te3elne	Bte3elne
Howwe	2a3lan	Yi3lon	Byi3lon
Hiyye	2a3lanit	Ti3lon	Bti3lon
Ento	2a3lanto	Te3elno	Bte3elno
Hinne	2a3lano	Ye3elno	Bye3elno
Ne7na	2a3lanna	Ni3lon	Mni3lon

	Imperative
2inta	3lon
2inte	3lene
2into	3leno

	Active Participle
Masculine	Mi3lin
Feminine	Mi3lne
Plural	Mi3lnin

Ana bo3lon isti2alit l 7okoome
I announce the resignation of the government

L 2asetze ra7 ye3elno l nateyij bokra
The teachers will announce the results tomorrow

2a3lanit l dawle eno bokra 3otle
The government announced that tomorrow is holiday

3leno l 2aseme ba2a!
Just announce the names!

Hinne mi3lnin eno bokra ra7 ysakro l mata3im
They have announced that tomorrow the restaurants will close

Turn red

	Perfect	Imperfect	Bi-imperfect
Ana	7marrit	2i7mar	Bi7mar
2inta	7marret	Ti7mar	Bti7mar
2inte	7marrayte	Ti7marre	Bti7marre
Howwe	7mar	Yi7mar	Byi7mar
Hiyye	7marrit	Ti7mar	Bti7mar
Ento	7marrayto	Ti7marro	Bti7marro
Hinne	7marro	Yi7marro	Byi7marro
Ne7na	7marrayna	Ni7mar	Mni7mar

	Imperative
2inta	7marr
2inte	7marre
2into	7marro

	Active Participle
Masculine	Mi7marr
Feminine	Mi7marra
Plural	Mi7marrin

Ana dighre bi7mar lamma 7ada yitghazzal fiyye
I turn red quick when someone flirts with me

Howwe ma lezim yi7mar lamma ydefi3 3an 7a22o
He should not turn red when he defends his rights

Hiyye 7marrit lamma jeboula akel b balesh
She turned red when they get her food for free

7marr shway la tfarji enak miste7e
Turn red a bit to show him that you are shy

Ma ba2a titghazal feyon lek kif mi7amarrin
Stop flirting with them look how they have turned red

To ascend

	Perfect	Imperfect	Bi-imperfect
Ana	Tlo3et	2itla3	Bitla3
2inta	Tlo3et	Titla3	Btitla3
2inte	Tlo3te	Titla3e	Btitla3e
Howwe	Toli3	Yitla3	Byitla3
Hiyye	Tol3it	Titla3	Btitla3
Ento	Tlo3to	Titla3o	Btitla3o
Hinne	Tol3o	Yitla3o	Byitla3o
Ne7na	Tlo3na	Nitla3	Mnitla3

Imperative	
2inta	Tla3
2inte	Tla3e
2into	Tla3o

Active Participle	
Masculine	Taali3
Feminine	Taal3a
Plural	Taal3in

Hiyye btitla3 3ala l jabal kel yom
She ascends to the mountain every day

Taali3 aw nezil?
Ascending or descending?

Tla3e la 3ande 3al taabi2 l telit
Ascend to me to the third floor

2imshe nitla3 nghayir jaw
Let's go have a good time

Tlo3to la 3anda 3al bet aw ba3ed?
Have you ascended (went up) to her home or not yet?

To turn

	Perfect	Imperfect	Bi-imperfect
Ana	Baramit	2ibrom	Bibrom
2inta	Baramit	Tibrom	Btibrom
2inte	Baramte	Teberme	Bteberme
Howwe	Baram	Yibrom	Byibrom
Hiyye	Baramit	Tibrom	Btibrom
Ento	Baramto	Tebermo	Btebermo
Hinne	Baramo	Yebermo	Byebermo
Ne7na	Baramna	Nibrom	Mnibrom

	Imperative
2inta	Brom
2inte	Breme
2into	Bremo

	Active Participle
Masculine	Berim
Feminine	Berme
Plural	Bermin

Baramit b 2arde w rje3et
I turned from where I am and went back

Ma lezim teberme b hal ser3a
You shouldn't turn that fast

Metel l bsaynet, byebermo deghre eza sem3o shi
Like cats, they turn immediately if they heat something

Brom w 7kine bwijje!
Turn and talk to my face!

L 2ossa manna mazboota, hiyye berme l 2ossa kella sawa
The story is not correct, she has turned the whole story around

To like

	Perfect	Imperfect	Bi-imperfect
Ana	7abbet	7ib	B7ib
2inta	7abbet	T7ib	Bit7ib
2inte	7abbayte	T7ibbe	Bit7ibbe
Howwe	7ab	Y7ib	Bi7ib
Hiyye	7abbit	T7ib	Bit7ib
Ento	7abbayto	T7ibbo	Bit7ebbo
Hinne	7abbo	Y7ibbo	Bi7ebbo
Ne7na	7abbayna	N7ib	Min7ib

Imperative	
2inta	7ib
2inte	7ibbe
2into	7ibbo

Active Participle	
Masculine	7aabib
Feminine	7abbe
Plural	7abbin

Ana ktir b7ib l koosa ma7shi
I like stuffed zucchinis a lot

Eh, howe 7abba lal benet
Yes, he liked the girl

Lezim n7ib ba3edna b hal balad
We should like each other in this country

7ibbo ba3ed!
Like each other!

Tal3a 7abbito w ma 5abbaritne!
She appears to has liked him and didn't tell me!

To order

	Perfect	Imperfect	Bi-imperfect
Ana	2amarto	2o2mor	Bo2mor
2inta	2amarit	To2mor	Bto2mor
2inte	2amarte	To2omre	Bto2omre
Howwe	2amar	Yo2mor	Byo2mor
Hiyye	2amarit	To2mor	Bto2mor
Ento	2amarto	To2omro	Bto2omro
Hinne	2amaro	Yo2omro	Byo2omro
Ne7na	2amarna	No2mor	Mno2mor

Imperative	
2inta	2mor
2inte	2more
2into	2moro

	Active Participle
Masculine	2emir
Feminine	2emra
Plural	2emrin

Ana ma b7ib 2o2mor, bas jible may 3mol ma3roof
I don't like to order, but get me water please

Sho 2amarte habibte?!
What did you order honey?!

Hiyye bto2mor w ne7na minnaffiz
She orders and we do

2morne 5ayye sho m3awiz?
Order me brother what do you need?

Howwe 2emir eno yi5las l malaf bokra
He has ordered for the file to be done by tomorrow

To wake up

	Perfect	Imperfect	Bi-imperfect
Ana	Fe2et	Fee2	Bfee2
2inta	Fe2et	Tfee2	Bitfee2
2inte	Fi2te	Tfee2e	Bitfee2e
Howwe	Fe2	Yfee2	Bifee2
Hiyye	Fe2it	Tfee2	Bitfee2
Ento	Fe2to	Tfee2o	Bitfee2o
Hinne	Fe2o	Yfee2o	Bifee2o
Ne7na	Fe2na	Nfee2	Minfee2

	Imperative
2inta	Fee2
2inte	Fee2e
2into	Fee2o

	Active Participle
Masculine	Feyi2
Feminine	Fey2a
Plural	Fey2in

Ana lezim fee2 kel yom 3al 3ashra
I have to wake up every day at ten

Ma 3am bifee2 ma3e, ghatis bel nawme 3al 2e5ir!
He's not waking up, he's in deep sleep

Fe2o kellon yalla ta3e 5edina
They all woke up, come pick us up

Fee2e bokra 3al tmene w ta3e nitrawwa2 sawa
Wake up tomorrow at eight and let's have breakfast together

Ta3ben ktir, feyi2 min l 5amse l sobo7
I'm very tired, I have been awake since five in the morning

Be able to

	Perfect	Imperfect	Bi-imperfect
Ana	2deret	2e2dar	Bi2dar
2inta	2deret	Ti2dar	Bti2dar
2inte	2dirte	Ti2dare	Bti2dare
Howwe	2eder	Yi2dar	Byi2dar
Hiyye	2idrit	Ti2dar	Bti2dar
Ento	2derto	Ti2daro	Bti2daro
Hinne	2edro	Yi2daro	Byi2daro
Ne7na	2derna	Ni2dar	Mni2dar

	Imperative
2inta	2daar
2inte	2dare
2into	2daro

	Active Participle
Masculine	2aadir
Feminine	2aadra
Plural	2aadrin

2deret 2i2na3o 2ennlo lle 3am ya3emlo ghalat
I was able to convince him that what he's doing is wrong

Eza baddo byi2dar ywa22if l sheghel kello
If he wants to, he is able to stop the whole work

Ana lezim 2e2dar seer 2i7ke
I have to be able to talk

Ma 5asne eza ma fik ti7mela, 2dar
Not my business if you can't lift it up, be able to

L sha3eb 2aadir ysa22it kil l zo3ama eza bado
The people are able to take down leader if they want to

Be born

	Perfect	Imperfect	Bi-imperfect
Ana	5le2et	2i5la2	Bi5la2
2inta	5le2et	Ti5la2	Bti5la2
2inte	5li2te	Ti5la2e	Bti5la2e
Howwe	5ele2	Yi5la2	Byi5la2
Hiyye	5il2it	Ti5las	Bti5la2
Ento	5le2to	Ti5la2o	Bti5la2o
Hinne	5el2o	Yi5la2o	Byi5la2o
Ne7na	5le2na	Ni5la2	Mni5la2

	Imperative
2inta	5laa2
2inte	5la2e
2into	5la2o

	Active Participle
Masculine	5al2aan
Feminine	5al2aane
Plural	5al2aaneen

Lal marra l tenye, b7ib 2i5la2 b libnen
For the next time, I would like to be born in Lebanon

7assit 7ala ka2ano 5il2it min jdid
She felt like she was born again

Libnen 3am yi5la2 min jdid w ne7na 3am ni5la2 ma3o
Lebanon is being reborn and we are being born with him

Ana 5al2aan b 7ay ktir fa2eer b Beirut
I was born in a very poor neighborhood in Beirut

Hinne bi7esso 7alon byi5la2o 3an jdid bas ti7keyon hek
They feel than they are born again when you talk to them like that

Outro

I hope you have all enjoyed the content of this book and will help you reach the goals you are aiming for!

I would be happy if you would like to check out my further work on all my YouTube channels: MatarTV, MatarEducation and MatarPodcast.

If you have any questions or feedback, please DM me on Instagram under: MatarTV.

Thank you again for buying this book and I hope I was able to give you some kind of value.

Stay safe and....
Yo2borne Alla!

Made in the USA
Las Vegas, NV
05 May 2021